A Living Faith
Miracles do happen

Pastor Steven Teo

Re-Gen

For the regeneration of our generation

A Living Faith
Miracles do happen

Copyright @ 2014 Re-Gen Ministries Inc.
Cover Design: Kim Valerio
Back Photo: Enzo Maisano

National Library of Australia Cataloguing-in-Publication

Teo, Steven, 1952- .
A living faith; miracles do happen

1st ed.
ISBN 9780977518067 (pbk.)

1. Miracles. I. Re-Gen Ministries Inc. II. Title.

231.73

Published by
Re-Gen Ministries Inc.

Dedication

To Ranon and Caelyn, my grand children who are the
epitome of miracles

And

To those who discovered the blessing of the miraculous,
seeing the unseen and continuing to call the things that are
not as though they were

I celebrate you all!

From the Author

This book has been on my heart for a long time. I have been in ministry for the last eleven years now and the experience of this incredible journey with the living faith has been bubbling within me since.

This is the experience of witnessing, engaging in and celebrating the miraculous in the lives of many individuals across the globe with whom I have had the privilege of meeting and ministering. From a definitive healing touch of God, the renewal of a mentally deranged mind to mundane things like the re-discovering a "lost" keychain password, I saw and experienced the invisible hand of God.

Though my training and background lends a natural inclination to the rational perspective of logic and economy, my experience with the faith journey has helped me thoroughly enjoy the spiritual. I am at home in both worlds being supernaturally natural yet naturally supernatural! I enjoy the spiritual as much as its practical application. Hence there is such a compulsion to write this book and explore the living faith and how it can apply to you and indeed for our society today.

If you are one of the many people agonizing with persistent issues and challenges that require a miracle to happen, keep in mind that God owns the process of the miraculous. Do not give up hope because God has proven to be far beyond anything anyone could envisage.

I encourage you to read the entire book to draw out your faith in expecting and seeing the impossible happen. The possibilities of the future that God has for you are immeasurably more than what you think or imagine.

Contents

Chapter 1

Miracles Do Happen

We are often greatly inspired by stories of how people who experienced miracles. They battled against great odds in their health, pain, setback, difficult background and upbringing or other struggles to receive what might have been seemingly impossible.

These are people whose lives appear to have been dealt a heavy blow and meted thoroughly disadvantageous positions which they certainly did not ask for; where situations appear to be virtually impossible and they have every reason to succumb to their circumstances. Yet there is an eventual breakthrough. Something miraculously happened. They are healed. They are set free. They have obtained what appears to be impossibility. They no longer need to endure their disabilities or the disadvantages. They are a walking miracle.

These people appear to be the favoured ones. They have inspiring stories to tell making them the envy of others.

Have you ever wondered why others seem to have all the miraculous things happening in their lives? These people appear to be the favoured ones. They have inspiring stories to tell making them the envy of others.

Have you ever asked yourself, "Why are the super specials not happening in my life?"

I believe desert phenomena like those experienced by ancient Israelites are parallels for our contemporary times – more so as our modern society degenerates by the day with political, media and other pressures being applied from every which corners to dilute the authenticity and truth of the Gospel.

This is precisely the time for believers to gear up their spirituality. Our society is not unspiritual; it is simply ungodly. For example, the New Age belief system is the fastest growing religion in Australia. We are witnessing a fondness for things spiritual within our nation, whether it is in witchcraft, the occult, the obsession with ghost hunting or simply the practice of exotic mystical religions. The Apostle Paul in writing to young Timothy best describes all these spirituality, *"Having a form of godliness but denying its power."*[1]

People have an innate craving for the supernatural. There is a vacuum in the hearts of human beings longing after the invisible and the miraculous. In essence it is really the deep longings for God the creator. God placed it there. The Psalmist knew this very well when he cried, *"My soul yearns, even faints, for the courts of the Lord; my heart and my flesh cry out for the living God."*[2]

Correcting Blind Spots

If we keep the miraculous out of our faith then our beliefs are no better than some talkfest. We therefore do not offer people something they are naturally built for. Inevitably people would seek the alternatives such as the like of Harry Potter, the psychics, the clairvoyants and even indulging in satanic practices.

Believers in every generation and culture have their own particular or even peculiar challenges. I call these "blind spots". One of the most obvious "blind spots" in the Western world today is the lack of understanding and experiencing of miracles within our daily existence. It is not something we would look out for or expect to see as a natural consequence of our situations. Perhaps it could be that we are having the good life with all the comfort, convenience and access to world-class facilities and so our default mode is not to access heaven for a miracle but to trot along the predictable for a human solution. This is unlike many parts of the Third World where resources and facilities are minimal. For example in the absence of adequate medical support, people naturally look to God for their healing and wholeness.

One of the results of the modern outlook is the decline in the belief of the intervening hand of an invisible God. Our lack of a miracle may not be due to God's inability or unwillingness but it may be because we are not actively looking for one! We may have allowed the mundane and routine to so dominate our lives to the exclusion of the supernatural.

Miracles do happen. Many of us may have failed to see that miracles do occur and often in the seemingly insignificant moments of our lives. Start expecting God to do wonders in your life. Miracles may appear random at times but that is not the case. Someone, somewhere has been believing and expecting. A seed must be first planted.[3]

For the last eleven years of my life, I have the privilege of travelling and ministering in many parts of the globe. I have met people of varying background and age who have had a miracle in their lives. These miracles range from the very mundane to life-threatening situations but in each situation the miraculous happened and they are a living testimonies and inspiration for me.

Our lack of a miracle may not be due to God's inability or unwillingness but it may be because we are not actively looking for one!

Their lives and their stories are not easily available in part because many of them are individuals who seek no recognition, accolade, fame or fortune. They quietly go about their lives with little fuss or the need even for acknowledgement.

This book is an attempt to tell their stories. Many of their names are not mentioned, as the essence of their story is to glorify the Lord God of their living faith. These stories are told with these intentions: Firstly to recount their miraculous happenings so that you, my reader will be blessed and inspired to discover the power of your own living faith; secondly to encourage you to look for the invisible hand of God in your own situation and thirdly, to give you invaluable insights on the workings of an all-powerful and purposeful supernatural God.

I am trusting that this book will go a long way to help you progress to being naturally supernatural in your life. Start by discovering the joy of being thrilled with the little things in life, recognizing the small miracles. It will change your perspective and lead you on the road to a miracle-filled life.

As you embrace the miraculous, never fear spirituality or be wary of it because there may be possible disappointment or dashed hopes if you expect a miracle and it did not happen. You must learn to look for it and see it happen. God is still the one *"who gives life to the dead and calls into being things that were not"*.[4]

"There are only two ways to live your life. One is as though nothing is a miracle. The other is as though everything is a miracle."

Albert Einstein

Chapter 2

The Importance Of Seeing

Some people can stare for hours at pictures where the subject matter is blended into the scenery with little result. And when someone points out the image they are supposed to see, it is almost embarrassing because right there in plain view the image is starring back at them! Theologian Stanley Hauerwas wisely said, "We do not see reality by just opening our eyes."[5] We often do not see what we are meant to see. And because we do not see, God cannot give it to us.

This is absolutely true with the miraculous. We do not experience the miraculous because we do not perceive it or we simply cannot see it happen. What you are able to conceive in your mind and the resulting expectation has a huge impact on the manner in which you shape your life, ministry and the way you accept and interact with spiritual phenomena in your walk with God.

This was evident in the life of the great Old Testament character, Moses. Scriptures tell us that, *"By faith Moses, when he had grown up refused to be known as the son of Pharaoh's daughter. He chose be mistreated along with the people of God rather than to enjoy the pleasures of sin for a short time. He regarded disgrace for the sake of Christ as of greater value than the treasures of Egypt, because he was looking ahead to his reward. By faith he left Egypt, not fearing the king's anger, he persevered because he saw him who is invisible."[6]*

Moses was able to give up life in a palace to live like a slave, chose to be mistreated, chose to live in disgrace over the treasures of Egypt because he saw what others did not see! He was able to risk his life again and again because he perceived the reality of God in a manner that is not neutral or natural. He saw the invisible supernatural God who had the ability and willingness to intervene on behalf of the oppressed ancient Israelites.

We often do not ask because we do not see. We cannot see it happening.

Without seeing, even the smallest problem in life will trip you and I. Even the tiniest issue will keep us from reaching our desired goals. If we can see it God will give it to us. The Apostle James says, "*You do not have, because you do not ask.*"[7] We often do not ask because we do not see. We cannot see it happening. We have no picture or vision of God intervening in our difficult situations; hence we do not even attempt to ask or seek for a miracle. As a result we live far short of our potential and we deny ourselves an avenue of experiencing spiritual phenomena in our Christian living.

Let me share with you what I believe Moses saw – a perception so powerful that it allowed him to walk away from everything that matters to his existence, first as a prince of Egypt but also notwithstanding rejection by his own people into desert phenomena and supernatural experiences with God.

Moses Saw his Identity

Moses saw who he was in the eyes of God. He saw what God had made him to be and his ultimate destiny. We are not what the world sees us to be. We are not what our families, friends, teachers or colleagues see us to be. What counts is what God sees us to be. To see your identity, you need to beg these questions;

Who are you? What has God made you to be? What has God called you to be? What has God destined you to be?

Moses fled Egypt and dwelt in the wilderness for 40 years. It was such a long time that when God came calling, he was unsure, had no confidence, no faith in the extraordinary. He had forgotten about his sense of purpose and calling. The first thing God did was to open his mind's eye and cause him to "see" his identity – and so by a miraculous faith he saw and then *"he refused to be known as the son of Pharaoh's daughter"*

Unless you see your sense of purpose and destiny, you will not do extraordinary exploits for God or experience the miraculous with God. You need to know your identity in order to determine what you could do and allow what God proposes to do in your life.

It won't work the other way around. Otherwise if what you do were taken away, you would feel like nobody. Think about famous people – artist, sportsmen, film stars and celebrities when they can no longer do what they do; they lose their individual bearings don't they? Many do not even begin to understand who they are! Many get depressed, even suicidal. This is because their identities depend solely on what they do!

It is time to see who you really are in Christ. You are more than conquerors. You are overcomers. God has treasures in store for you, things that the eyes have not seen, the ears have not heard or has it entered into your hearts.[8] God has plans to prosper you, not to harm you, to give you hope and a future.[9]

Allow the Holy Spirit to open your mind and begin to "see" your true identity and calling

Unless you see your sense of purpose and destiny, you will not do extraordinary exploits for God or experience the miraculous with God.

in Christ. Do not let anyone or anything take that away from you. With that identity you will do extra ordinary exploits and experience the living faith.

Moses Saw his Reward

When Moses was forty years old, the prince took upon himself the role of a liberator. On day, he chanced upon an unmerciful Egyptian guard beating a Hebrew slave. Moses sprang to the defense of the Hebrew and in the commotion he killed the guard.

God showed him the aura of leadership, the promise and thrill of signs and wonders.

He thought that he could get away with the killing as he was among his people. After all he was helping his fellow Hebrews, a people that were heavily oppressed by the Egyptians. However within a very short time, the same people made it known that there were not interested in his help or leadership. When he tried to intervene in a subsequent quarrel among them, they told him off in no uncertain terms. Most of us would have known the story; Moses had to flee for his life. Suddenly he was the criminal, wanted by the Egyptian authorities, not the leader he envisaged.[10] He lost everything. He forfeited his access to power and wealth, lost all his princely reputation and whatever nobility or social position he had acquired in the kingdom.

So years later when God finally caught up with him in the burning bush,[11] he became the greatest procrastinator ever! He was not the least interested in his previous life. He no longer had the passion of standing up for his fellow Hebrews or entertained any notion of liberating his people.

But God changed all that by causing him to "see" his reward. The scriptures say, *"He regarded disgrace for the sake of Christ as greater value than the treasures of Egypt,"* Why did Moses change his view about how out of touch he was with the reality of his existence? *"Because he was looking for his reward."* God showed him the aura of leadership, the promise and thrill of signs and wonders[12] and the new Moses saw and resonated with his earlier vision. He saw that God had something extraordinary for him, a feat or an exploit for him to do and that there were just rewards for him. Moses saw and knew then that God is a rewarder.[13]

The rest is history. Moses led his people out of Egypt. He liberated his people from Egyptian oppression. The very people who rejected him subsequently made him their greatest hero. He still owns a large piece of Jewish history.

King David in the Old Testament had a similar idea of God being the rewarder. Right from his tender age, young David knew that God has rewards in exploits and that He would turn up for his people in extra ordinary fashion. When he stumbled on Goliath bad-mouthing his nation and God, David knew an exploit was at hand; he just did not know what was the reward.

So *"David asked the men standing near him, "What will be done for the man who kills this Philistine and removes this disgrace from Israel?"*[14] For David killing Goliath was a given. He knew God would do the job as he had witnessed similar feats on the lion and bear which were attacking his sheep.[15] The Philistine giant was a non-issue. Instead what interested him was the reward embedded in the miraculous. He saw his reward. He saw his miracles!

15

Moses Saw the Invisible

Before Moses could undertake the difficult task of leading and breaking the ancient Israelites out of Egyptian bondage the scriptures say, *"He saw him who is invisible"*. And so *"by faith he forsook Egypt, not fearing the King's anger; he persevered because he saw him who is invisible."*

Moses saw the invisible God first, then obeyed and did the impossible.[16] The internal picture or photograph of what is invisible to the naked eye changed him from a stuttering, faltering and now unbelieving person to an extraordinary proclaiming, believing and faith person who is now equipped and empowered to do the impossible both in Egypt as well as the journey through the wilderness of the Middle East.[17]

Our biggest challenge in contemporary society is the willingness to "see" the invisible hand of the awesome God. This means that we have to put aside preconceived notions in our upbringing, our mindset, our fears and apprehensions. We need to see with the eyes of our heart, refusing to be impaired by the limitations of our past, the cultural indifferences or the difficulties of the present. Instead we need to see the possibilities of the future where a miracle is going to settle issues for us.

Our biggest challenge in contemporary society is the willingness to "see" the invisible hand of the awesome God.

We must see our invisible God and his intervening hand within our daily existence. We must see the mandate and authority God has given us. This mandate and authority would allow us to walk boldly in the Holy Spirit's anointing. Failure to see the invisible is a major hindrance to God's blessing and miracle.

The Gospel has an interesting passage where scriptures demonstrated this principle of seeing the invisible.[18] The people in Jesus' hometown were not able to experience and witness miracles. This was because they kept seeing Jesus as the carpenter's son. What they saw, they were offended in some ways and so Jesus did not do many miracles. The people saw the obvious and the familiar. They saw him not as the Son of God but the son of Mary. They saw him like his earthly brothers and sisters and what they see was what they got.

It was not that the Saviour lacked compassion for his own folks. It was not that Jesus had less power or authority in his hometown. In effect he was constrained by what the people perceived in their minds and hearts.

The manner in which they saw Jesus affected their belief and expectations, so the seed for the miraculous was not sown in the first place. No wonder even the Saviour was unable to do much for his community.

Walk In Faith

Oral Roberts says, "We live by faith or die by doubt".[19] Faith is the absolute essential to experiencing the miraculous. It is the necessary ingredient for a taste of the supernatural.

A living faith is core to our Christian life. In our journey with God, we see in faith, we ask in faith, we receive in faith and we obey in faith. If there is no faith, there is no tomorrow, there is no life and there is no hope. The Christian life is a journey of faith.

This is the essence of faith – our ability to trust God.

Faith is what God responds to. Without it, it is impossible to please God.[20]Without faith nothing happens. All we have got then is fear, uncertainty and worry.

When we say that we have faith in

someone, what does that mean? It usually means that we see the invisible qualities in the person; hence we have no reason to disbelieve the individuals. We take him at his words. We trust him. Faith therefore sees the invisible God and believes God's word. Faith believes the promises of God.

This is the essence of faith – our ability to trust God. Allow the Holy Spirit to supernaturally empty the doubts in your life and commence a new perspective of seeing and expecting the miraculous. It is so important for us to see. It is incredible how when our inside is changed, that the outside begins to conform to what is on the inside. Try it – and start a new living faith.

"We see the world, not as it is, but as we are"

Talmud

Chapter 3

The Road To Emmaus

Remember the story of the two gentlemen on the road to Emmaus in the Gospel of Luke? There they were on their way to Emmaus, a small town about twelve kilometers from Jerusalem. They were followers of Christ heading out of town not realizing that Jesus was resurrected. They like many of the disciples obviously weren't seeing or believing what Jesus had taught them about his death and resurrection!

The two disciples had followed and risked their lives for Jesus the Nazarene and now he was crucified and buried. They were dismayed at the events transpiring in recent times. They were crestfallen and disheartened. They lost all hope and in their minds and hearts had all the reasons to be disappointed and dispirited. As they trudged back toward their homes, scriptures tell us that the resurrected Jesus sneaked alongside, incognito, and joined in their discouraged conversations. Jesus pretended to be ignorant of what has been happening and they did not recognise him.

The two disciples were too engrossed with their sense of loss to notice whether he was a friend or an acquaintance. They simply assumed he was a stranger. In their being carried away by the unfolding events. they demonstrated a lack of belief or expectation that the Nazarene would be raised from the dead in three days.

Jesus played the game really well. He feigned ignorance by asking them, *"What are you discussing together as you walk along?" "They stood still, their faces downcast. One of them, named Celopas, asked him, "Are you only a visitor to Jerusalem and do not know the things that have happened there in these days?" "What things?" he asked. "About Jesus of Nazareth." They replied. "He was a prophet, powerful in word and deed before God and all the people. The chief priests and our rulers handed him over to be sentenced to death, and they crucified him; but we had hoped that he was the one who was going to redeem Israel."* [21]

The two disciples not only did not see, they had no expectation of the miraculous whatsoever. The most awesome miracle of the resurrected Christ had taken place, right in the heart of Jerusalem, right in their midst and they had no idea at all. Their inability or failure to see or to expect the supernatural led to their decision to head for home – back to their previous existence, closing a big chapter of their lives.

The sad thing about our generation is that unbelief in the miraculous is the least resistant path to our belief system.

We live in a time of great miraculous happenings. People across Asia, Africa and Latin America have often reported that they witnessed the miraculous. Some are simple. Others are complex. Some miracles are undoubtedly questionable but others appear indisputable. Signs of the cross and crosses of light have shown up all around the world. Some look as though a slide machine projected them on the faces of buildings, on windowpanes, and on objects. Others appear to be suspended in mid air.[22] I had a friend who witnessed a cross appearing on his mobile phone at a Cell Meeting one night and he promptly showed it to the group gathered there. He had it photographed before it disappeared and then texted it over to me. It is still sitting in my mobile phone. It is no figment of his imagination as this friend is a levelheaded successful businessman in his profession.

The sad thing about our generation is that unbelief in the miraculous is the least resistant path to our belief system. It is hard to accept or believe in a miracle, as if it is viewed as an unacceptable norm of modern culture.

And what were the reasons for the two disciples' inability to perceive or see Jesus or the circumstances they were in? I believe there are three things that plagued their minds and hearts – and these are as valid today as they were in Biblical times.

The manner in which you are beholden to him in your heart is the manner in which your life is positioned to witness the miraculous God has in store for you.

Blinded Eyes

Firstly, the two travellers were clearly blinded. They did not recognize Jesus. They thought he was a stranger. It is interesting that the scriptures did not say why they were blinded – if indeed it was God or the Devil or their own extent of grief and sense of loss that blinded their eyes.[23] Maybe Luke the writer left the details out for a reason; to show the lack of expectation or anticipation on the part of the two disciples.

The Gospel of Luke is often known as the social Gospel. Even the boyhood of Jesus was recorded with more details than any other Gospel. The writer was careful to write about Jesus meeting societal needs, particularly the needs of the poor and the Christian obligation and relationship with society at large. A distinctive feature of this Gospel is the strong emphasis on accountability as stewards of God. He would have commented on how the two travellers did not understand the issue at hand.

22

After all, the entire unfolding event was the talk of the town! Who would have missed it?

So Luke may have intended for us to ponder the many ways we understand and see Jesus without ever really understanding or seeing Him. Some of us may indeed see Jesus as a Political and Social Reformer or a moral person or a good and just man or merely a prophet of God. History certainly carries numerous views of who Jesus was! Our modern world has many distorted opinions of who Jesus is.

But how are you seeing Jesus? Do you see him as an earthly historical figure or a swear word as many Australians do or merely a prophet, a good and just man, or are you seeing that Jesus is the Lord and Saviour, the author and finisher of your faith? The manner in which you are beholden to him in your heart is the manner in which your life is positioned to witness the miraculous God has in store for you.

Burning Hearts

The two disciples did not see or expect anything more than the ordinary in part because they ignored the secret of their burning hearts.[24] They subsequently asked each other, *"Were not our hearts burning within us while he talked with us on the road and opened the scriptures to us?"*[25]

Jesus scolded them for being *"slow of heart to believe"*.[26] In other words the two were not seeing with the eyes of their hearts. He reminded them of the writing of the prophets, began to walk them through the not so obvious in the scriptures and all the ancient wisdom there is. Then out of courtesy, they invited him for supper as it was getting late. Now I want you to listen

They reminisced how their hearts were burning or aflame as it were when Jesus was conversing with them on the journey home.

23

carefully to what the scriptures have to say: *"When he was at the table with them, he took bread, gave thanks, broke it and began to give it to them. Then their eyes were opened and they recognized him and he disappeared from their sight.*[27]

In that powerful instantaneous moment the two travellers recognized Jesus their Saviour and Lord! As the scales fell from their eyes, they remembered, then they saw the reality of God in their midst. They reminisced how their hearts were burning or set aflame as it were when Jesus was conversing with them on the journey home.

I believe God gave us this story for a purpose, so that we carry an expectation within our hearts for the miraculous things of God. The story is to remind us that things may not be what they seem, that our reading of the many unfolding events in life may leave a serious gap between perception and reality. We live in two worlds or rather, in one world with two parts the one part that we can see with our natural eyes and the other part we can see with the eyes of our heart.[28] We live in the natural world but we also live in the spiritual world. We must learn to see with our natural eyes and correspondingly we must see with our spiritual eyes. We see and expect the supernatural when we see with the eyes of our heart. The two travellers' visions were low but if they had paid attention, their hearts would have shown them the truth.[29] It was burning while it happened.

We see and expect the supernatural when we see with the eyes of our heart.

How we need to re-train and re-wire the way we see and feel. How wonderful it is that the Holy Spirit often burns within our hearts – allowing and helping us to see what is not readily available to the natural mind. Ask the Holy Spirit to fill you with a *"state of knowing that you know that you know"*; expect him to give you this knowing faith inside you as you draw from the miraculous within your life.[30]

God Owns the Process

In many of the strategy and thought leadership work[31] that I conduct with professional individuals, businesses and churches I try to help people understand the principle of "cause and effect" relationship. *"Because of that, now this is the effect."* Hence, because you failed to seek new skills, now you are left behind without a new and better job. Because you skipped all the classes, now you are struggling in your exams. Because you ate too much and had poor eating habit, now you have a weighty problem. I call this a process-outcome model. Because of the processes you have in place within your life or for that matter, within your relationship, business or career, the outcome is fairly predictable. Outcome is the natural result of the processes we engage in.

Most people look for outcome instead of process, as it is far easier to conceptualize a great outcome. It is an easy way out, effortless and without causing too much grief and strife. However if the processes are incorrect or inappropriate, the outcome is often different to our expectation. Too often we expect to go north but our processes take us south. We expect little and then we wonder why God fails to miraculously turn up for us.

We agonize through the twists and turns of our lives without realizing or are realising too slow that God owns the process.

The focus on process is not an easy behavior. It can be harsh and unforgiving. It extracts a lot out of us. The process journey may be too long and disheartening. I have met people who knew what they have to do to bring situations in their lives to an even keel but they would not because it was just too hard. The discipline of process is a

25

difficult one and many avoid it altogether to their own detriment.

Truth is, we agonize through the twists and turns of our lives without realizing or are realising too slow that God owns the process. Tough as it were for our existence, God owns all the processes in our lives, the ups and the downs, the good times and the bad times. He rules in the affairs of man![32] He knows the past, the present and the future. He is the same yesterday, today and forever.[33] He sees the big picture. He knows with certainty what lies ahead.

We on the other hand, we only know what we know – a limited view of our existence but we often act as if we know everything, don't we? We are too smart for our own good. So we see a certain situation and we draw an immediate predictable conclusion. Like the two travellers who saw the crucifixion as the end of Jesus, who also saw the power of the Roman Empire and what they could do if you were not in compliance, and they concluded that all was lost and started a journey reverting to their former lives.

Dejected, downcast having lost all hope. They thought they had staked it all on Jesus the Nazarene and now he was dead. So they drooped back toward their old ways – ready to quit, to revert to their previous vocation and to surrender their destiny. The process of believing and expecting the impossible was simply too difficult to appropriate or comprehend.

God was still calling what is not as though they were.

But God was not through yet with them – he owns the process. There is more to what meets their eyes. God was still calling what is not as though they were.[34] Because God owns the process, you and I can sit comfortably knowing that the outcome is going to be good and that his purposes would dominate every facet of our lives. There are no mistakes with God.

He owns the process, more so given the complexity and sophistication of our contemporary existence. Since he owns the process, we need simply to enjoy the outcome. The Apostle Paul understood this very well when he says *"And we know that in all things God works for the good of those who love him, who have been called according to his purpose."*[35]

Too Clever For Our Own Good

As a generation we are too clever for our own good, which also explains why our modern world is so at odds with God. We take his silence for his death and we ignore him at every which turn. We have in this modern world, everything that comfort and technology could possibly give yet there exist a highest ever depression and suicide rate, extreme wickedness, random crimes, atrocities and ever-escalating divorce rate with dysfunctional families and people! And we wonder why with all our modern laws, humanistic beliefs and advanced technology we are going backwards not forward.

What if you just relax, craft an expectation in your heart and let God be God. Let God show you his glory – expect a miracle, relax and trust him for the supernatural intervening hand of God in your difficult situation. You would be surprised how fast the perception and reality starts to marry in your life and for the miraculous to abound.

We take his silence for his death and we ignore him at every which turn.

Be careful not to draw conclusions about your life or your situation that may not be based on fact or truth or what the Word of God says. The two disciples – their eyes were dim, their understandings fell short but if they had paid attention, their hearts would have shown them the profound truth. They would have been anticipating and experiencing the resurrection miracle. No wonder scriptures tell us, *"Above all else, guard your heart, for everything you do flows from it."*[36]

"Miracles are a retelling in small letters of the very same story which is written across the whole world in letters too large for some of us to see."

C.S. Lewis

Chapter 4

No More Back Pain

The backdrop to this amazing story was Indonesia. I was the camp speaker for an English-speaking congregation in North Jakarta. The pastors were veteran Singaporean missionaries.[37]

The camp was held at Puncak, up in the mountains around 80km from the City of Jakarta. It was an awesome time of divine visitation and the Lord touched many. Five of the campers were filled with the Holy Spirit. A couple of campers were healed of their sicknesses - one lady was able to cross her legs for the first time in many months and another was able to sleep really well (and missed breakfast the next morning!) after suffering countless difficulties and sleepless nights before. I went away from the ministry fulfilled and enriched. That was in August 2006.

It is extremely difficult to speak year-on-year in a camp situation as you would have inevitably shared your best sermons, said the best jokes and used the best illustrations.

Around June 2007, I received an invitation by the same pastors asking me to be their family camp speaker again and they cheekily suggested that it "was by popular demand". This was a back-to-back arrangement for which I was most reluctant. It is extremely difficult to speak year-on-year in a camp situation as you would have inevitably shared your best sermons, said the best jokes and used the best illustrations. It is a demanding task indeed and so I hesitated in responding to the invitation.

Shortly later, I received an email from a Filipino expatriate who was working as a teacher in Jakarta and had attended the 2006 camp I ministered in. She was the lady who was healed of her back pain; the one who was then able to cross her legs for the first time in many months. She wrote excitedly and told the story of her healing and that months after the August camp, she remained completely healed. She wrote of her eagerness to see me again in the forthcoming camp. The email from Concepcion P. Solicito (Connie) was the necessary trigger for me to accept the second invitation for the engagement.

It was in Gunung Geulis, Bogor Indonesia that I met Connie again for the second time. She was in the pink of health. This is her story:

I have had a very bad posture. I tend to slouch most of the time. As a pre-school teacher, I also tend to squat or bend down when conversing with the children in my class. At first it did not bother me at all though I knew in the long run it would cause back pains – and it surely did!

During my first year in a pre-school, I handled toddlers (terrible twos!). Many times I had to carry one child for fifteen minutes to half hour to comfort him or her as two years old children are still by the way babies! Each session lasted for two and a half hours per day – a relatively short time but physically tiring.

This was the beginning of my back pain problems. At the end of the session, I would lie down on the carpet with small pillow under my back and I could really feel excruciating pains from time to time. This went on for a year, but I did not consult a doctor. I thought that perhaps it is because of my work. Instead, I prayed to be transferred to the higher-level class, as I know definitely that carrying children was not for me due to my small body frame.

God answered my prayers. The following year, the principal moved me to the oldest class level; Kindergarten 2, age level 5-6. My back pains had lessened. However in Kindergarten 2, I had to sit on the carpet cross leg when teaching most of the hands-on lessons to the children. As the years went by, my back pain was getting worse. I noticed that before I could sit long hours on a chair or cross leg on a carpet for many minutes, but this time, it takes only ten minutes and I can feel the pain.

I love sitting cross legs. It is my favourite prayer position as it keeps me more awake and alert during my morning and evening devotions with God. However, the longer I sat in that position the more agony of pain it was causing my back. It was really hard.

I was so scared and concerned. My Auntie was diagnosed with scoliosis and my sister Abigail with mild scoliosis. I feared I was becoming the third. I tried to exercise regularly to strengthen my back. It did help a bit but I cannot do sit-ups for it will really punish my back.

I subsequently had a bone density test for any possible signs of osteoporosis. The test result was normal. I was so relieved. I was still scared because I have read somewhere that scoliosis is one of a genetic disease. This troubled me thinking that my profession could have triggered it – my mind was running wild with paranoia!

In August 2006, our church invited Pastor Steven Teo to be the speaker for our annual church camp. Pastor Steven preached about living an abundant life which includes having

After the prayer I fell backwards on the floor, but as I was lying there, I felt something like heat flowing through my spinal cord and all over my back. It was a strange feeling.

a healthy life. The preaching was really practical and wonderful.

In one of our night meetings during the camp, Pastor Steven asked those who needed healing to come forward. He said, "I will pray for you". I was very sure that the Holy Spirit was leading him to do that as I felt an inner compulsion to go forward for the prayer. To be very honest, I was very hesitant. I was thinking and said to myself, "I am not sure what this pain is about, it could just be due to my bad posture and perhaps God will heal me with regular exercise." Deep within me however, I could feel the urgency to go forward so I finally yielded and stepped out.

As I was standing at the altar and it was my turn to be prayed for, Pastor Steven asked me which part of my body needed healing. I told him that I have been suffering from back pains. He touched my back and prayed for it. After the prayer I fell backwards on the floor, but as I was lying there, I felt something like heat flowing through my spinal cord and all over my back. It was a strange feeling. I had never felt or experienced it before. Soon I felt so much better.

I did not know if it was scoliosis or another problem or issue. I do not really care anymore. All I know was that the night after the meeting and the altar ministry, I prayed before going to bed, crossed my leg for more than half hour without any pain on my back! Praises to God the Healer!

When I last met Connie at the second camp, she was happy and well. Matter of fact, she was active in the camp, serving as a member of the registration team. I subsequently spoke to Connie about my writing a book on miracles and asked me if she could write her story to give glory to God and to inspire others to know that we do indeed have a living faith. Miracles do happen – and for her it was a wonderful one!

All glory to the living God!

"Miracles are like pimples, because once you start looking for them you find more than you ever dreamed you'd see."

Lemony Snicket, *The Lump of Coal*

Chapter 5

God Bless Us With A Child

This amazing story took place in Melaka (Malacca), Malaysia.[38] It is amazing because firstly there was obviously the intervening hand of God and secondly I have never seen or experienced divine appointment in such a pronounced and targeted manner.

I felt the need to minister in West Malaysia, in the states of Penang and Kedah but my primary objective was to return to the City of Klang to minister in the Sunday service of a pastor-friend's church.[39] This trip was meant to "compensate" him, as I was unable to minister at his church on a couple of previous ministry trips to the nation.

However the arrangement and crafting of my itinerary was left to a good friend in Penang, as I was busy with my work at Law School and the continuing ministry that I carried on most, if not all weekends within Australia. I had therefore assumed that the itinerary would include a Sunday meeting in Klang but instead I found myself ministering in Melaka for that particular weekend in August 2011.

The trip south was the last leg of an extended ministry in the Northern Malaysian towns of Ipoh, Sungai Petani, Chemor and Penang Island. But the trip to Melaka was unintended.

When I caught up with the pastor concerned in Klang, on my way down south to Melaka, I had to apologise for the miss again.

Nevertheless I had the opportunity to speak and minister to his leadership group around a steamboat dinner that night.

It was almost amusing to see the orchestrating hand of God in the unintended situation. In the afternoon, I was having a cup of coffee at the local coffee shop with the pastor when his mobile phone rang. On the line was the senior pastor of the Melakan church where I was scheduled to speak at the weekend. There was apparent apprehension over my coming, in part because I had never met the pastor. This was a third-party arrangement.

It was clear that the senior pastor was a little concerned about the forthcoming visiting minister. Over the phone, my friend was answering all the inevitable questions for a visiting speaker who is of unknown quality and untested. Looking at me, with a twinkle in his eyes, he said over the phone, "Pastor Steven is a great speaker. He'll do very well for you and the church. Don't worry."

And so it was that I turned up in Melaka wondering what God has in store for the people in the church. I have learnt, not always successfully though I must confess, that when things bungle up, often there is a Godly reason for it. It pays to exercise patience and to sit back, relax and see the glory of God manifesting itself!

It was almost amusing to see the orchestrating hand of God in the unintended situation.

On the Saturday morning, the senior pastor[40] took me out for breakfast.[41] I then met two of her leaders, both of whom are lawyers of a partnership practice in the city. In the course of our casual conversation, one of the lawyers told me of his futile seven-years wait for a child since marriage.

I could not recall what led to this particular topic but I immediately sensed in my spirit that this was the reason for my being found in the city and the church. I felt that it was a Godsent appointment and that something good was going to happen over the weekend.

For a start, I knew for all intent and purpose I was not even meant to be ministering in Melaka that weekend. But I immediately resonated with the gentlemen and his predicament. My wife and I had to wait till the eighth year of our marriage for our only child. I remember those seven long years of waiting, and the pain and disappointment we endured.

God wonderfully and miraculously provided us with a son.

God wonderfully and miraculously provided us with a son. My wife and I have been telling our story ever since. I have in fact written the story in my first book, *Destiny*.[42] Ever since this miraculous gift, I have been on special lookout to pray for people who are having difficulties in child bearing. In my travel and ministry, I have prayed for many in different parts of the world and the results have been most encouraging.

I then had the opportunity to interact more with the senior pastor who later shared that this issue had been a most discouraging factor for the couple, and that she and the church had been earnestly praying for them.

Altar ministry on a Sunday morning service is typically a time-consuming one for me. I would pray for people, one at a time often accompanied with words of encouragement or a prophetic word. Many people in the prayer queue are kind enough to wait a fair bit before I get to them. Conscious of the probability of that happening, I told the gentlemen to make sure he and his wife turn up for prayers on Sunday morning. So in a sense it was an arrangement for me to pray for the couple. I did that with the view that no matter how busy or forgetful I might be; the couple would come forward to ask for prayer.

The Sunday came. Predictably the altar was full and I took a long time to pray for individuals. The lawyer subsequently told me that he thought I might have forgotten – they were indeed the last to be prayed for. On that Sunday morning, Wong Fook Meng cried for the first time at an altar service. His spirit was so touched with the manifest presence of the living God.

I usually travel with some of my books. They are for sale and they generate income to assist in the expenses of the ministry. In this instance I ran out of them and in particular the book, *Destiny* where I wrote about our own miraculous gift of life. I promised and subsequently mailed a copy of the book to Fook Meng's wife and it was very much appreciated. The rest is history.

This is his story:

My wife and I had waited for about eight years to have a child. Despite many years of prayers, God appeared to be silent to our heart's longings. This had been especially difficult for my wife who loves children. She works as a principal of a childcare centre and sees it as her mission to love and teach children. Yet, it seems to us at that time that it may not be our privilege to hold a child of our own in our arms.

He (Pastor Steven) prayed that God bless us with a child. Two months later, (my wife) Joo Li was pregnant with Sophia Joy. All glory to God for His abundant grace.

We learnt through our experience with infertility that God's timing is impeccable. He orchestrated Pastor Steven's visit to our church at a time when we were most desperate for a supernatural intervention from God.

Miracles do happen. The Christian faith is indeed a living faith. The supernatural is meant to be a natural part of our existence. I had the privilege and opportunity to visit the church in Melaka again in 2013, held Sophia Joy in my arms and celebrated with the couple over the gift of life that God has bestowed on them.

When the child was born, there was much celebration, in the family as well as the community of church. The father was so pleased that he (on behalf of Sophia) wrote a special message to the congregation.

Sophia Joy's First Message to City Community Church dated 01.07.2012:

Hello everyone!

My name is Sophia Joy Wong. I am two days old. It feels great to finally see the light of day. It was pretty dark in mummy's womb for the past 9 months!

I just want to thank all of you for all your precious prayers for me. My daddy and mummy told me that I am the answer to many years of prayers, which were bathed in much tears. They said they waited very long for my arrival.

When Daddy held me for the first time yesterday and I looked into his eyes, he was just crying and crying. "Hey, I thought I was the baby!" Mummy was overjoyed too to see me. She fed me some milk yesterday. It tasted good but will be better if it comes in strawberry flavour.

Well, I look forward to getting to know all of you pretty soon! I hope to be running around in the church, sing children's praise songs, attend Sunday School and play with you in CGs and First Mondays and I know I will make my way into Daddy's sermons in the future.

I also hope that when you see me, you will remember that God answers prayers. And that He still works miracle. I am a living proof of that! So, whatever it is you are praying for, don't give up. It is always too soon to quit.

Lastly, my Daddy and Mummy say it takes a church to raise a child. So, I will look up to all of you as good examples...so, you better be good ya! I know I can count on you.

I hope to see you real soon. As I am sleeping most of the time, do pardon me if I don't wake up to greet you. And, I have got everything I need so you don't have to trouble yourself to bring any gift...but, if you really insist, I don't mind an iPad 3...he he he, just kidding! My Daddy says a Starbucks coffee for him will do just fine.

Love,
Sophia Joy Wong

All glory to the living God!

"You did not have to understand miracles to believe in them, and in fact Mabel had begun to suspect the opposite. To believe, perhaps you had to cease looking for explanations and instead hold the little thing in your hands as long as you were able before it slipped like water between your fingers."

Eowyn Ivey, *The Snow Child*

Chapter 6

We Are Expecting A Baby Boy

It was my first trip to Russia. It was cold. This was October 2005. Within a few hours of arriving in Moscow, after a twenty-eight hour marathon flight from Melbourne via Vienna, I was heading into the city of Pskov[43]

I was travelling with a team of Australian pastors but after a few preliminaries with our hosts, I was immediately driven alone to the train station. This was for an overnight twelve-hour train ride to Pskov. We were split into three groups for our respective places of ministry and mine was the group of one!

It was an exhaustive bumpy ride before I reached the city. My hosts had booked for a special two-bunk cabin and I immediately felt that I should be travelling alone without a stranger alongside me the whole night. I prayed. and indeed had the whole cabin to myself.

Arriving at Pskov was almost comical. As if the tension of not being able to speak a single word of Russian was not enough, I did not even know who was going to receive me at the train station. It was commotion everywhere. The train had hardly come to a halt when people were already piling on board, carrying luggage, bags and stuff off cabins. Adding to the chaos was booming voices everywhere. I suspect the Russians are somehow able to harness the natural resonances of their vocal tracts to a hilt! In the sea of confusion, a guy appeared from nowhere and grabbed my luggage, gesturing me to follow him. I had a shock but at least he looked friendly enough. He indicated non-verbally that he knew I was his man because I was the only Asiatic person there!

Ministry in Pskov was awesome. I ministered in two services on Sunday morning in a Pentecostal church.[44] I had a wonderful time in the presence of God. People were touched and healed by the Lord. Many were at the altar receiving the anointing of the Holy Spirit. The altar was full and many were in tears. In both services I saw spiritual gifting in operation.

I must admit my apprehension prior to the Russian ministry. Russia was the great unknown for me. I was not sure how the reception would be, particularly when I would be travelling alone and ministering in my own right. Those feelings were unfounded.

Not only were the Christians open and hungry for the Lord, my hosts in Pskov and the surrounding regions where I also carried ministry were most hospitable. They took good care of me. I had a wonderful place to stay. I was served excellently. The chef at the Bible School was a very good cook (I stayed at the School hostel in a visiting lecturer facility). She served brilliantly.

I thoroughly enjoyed ministering in the Bible School as well with an intensive on "Leadership". There were twenty students and I fell in love with all of them! One of the students testified to the healing of her backache. They were a wonderful bunch of people preparing to serve God in the fields. It was such a defining moment.

Throughout my ministry, I had great interpreters, individuals whose command of the English language was par excellence. One in particular was truly outstanding. She spoke with an American accent. She took her role seriously and was on my side at all times. Throughout the services and indeed elsewhere as well, she would be translating every conversation for me. It was like having a walking commentary. As a result I was well plucked in to my surrounds despite the language barrier. I knew what was spoken, what was discussed and how things were moving along.

At the altar, she was translating all the time. This was not easy as I was praying prophetically; giving scriptures and words flowed freely and swiftly. She was alongside, not missing a word. I could see the impact of her translation as individuals started to break down in tears and some were screaming in reaction to the word. Customary to my ministry, the altar work took a longer time than the norm but people stayed on, patiently waiting for their turn.

When it was all done, the interpreter asked if I wanted a glass of water. My voice was hoarse from the prayers. So we headed to the kitchen area together. There I was introduced to her husband, a huge man and a former military officer of the Soviet Army.

It was in the kitchen area that the interpreter together with her husband asked if I would pray for them. They briefly told me that they have been married for twelve years without a child. They asked if I would pray for the Lord's favour to be on their lives. I remember saying, "Of course!"

"This is the photograph of your future. This is the photograph of your son. See the future as God is showing a picture of it."

I held both their hands and began to pray. As I did the Lord impressed on my heart to pull my mobile phone out of my pocket and showed the couple a photograph of my son. I immediately stopped praying, pulled the hand phone out and showed them the

44

photograph of Joses, my son. I was stunned at what came out of my mouth right there and then. The thought was new to me. It was as if I was not the one speaking but the one listening. It was a word of knowledge.[45]

"See this picture," I said, "this is the photograph of your future. This is the photograph of your son. See the future as God is showing a picture of it." The poor girl began to cry and the awesome anointing came on us.

Unbeknown to me, the couple was trying to have a baby via artificial insemination. They kept quiet about the matter preferring to keep confidential their effort to have a child. The years of waiting must have been stressful and disappointing. They must have tried every conceivable means to have a baby but without success. Now they were spending money and time to invest into their future, hoping that science and all the medical expertise would assist them somehow.

I left Pskov for Moscow after more than a week of travelling and ministry. It was tiring but enjoyable altogether. My Russian experience had been good. It was not long before the Russian ministry was just memories as I moved on to other nations and ministries.

Now they were spending money and time to invest into their future, hoping that science and all the medical expertise would assist them somehow.

One day, an email appeared and in it my Russian interpreter had a story to tell:

Hello dear Pastor Steven!

The Galkins family is writing to you. We hope you remember your visit to Pskov last year.

I was translating for you in Pskov and in Ostrov. My name is Galya. You prayed for our family to have a baby and showed the picture of your son as our future. You asked us to inform you when we have some progress in this situation.

So with great joy we tell you that we are expecting the baby boy, it is five and the half months now. He must be born in January or beginning of February.

God is good to us. We were waiting for this miracle for 12 years. We always give thanks and glory to Him. If you are in Russia in winter, we invite you to our family. Also we ask you to pray for our precious baby.

We remembered you many times. We enjoyed your sermons in our region and I enjoyed translating for you. Thank you very much. God bless you and your family abundantly!

Galya

> *It is still the intervening hand of God that brought a prophetic assurance into their hearts that all was well.*

She is now a mother. How awesome is our God? The artificial insemination could have been responsible for her to conceive the baby but ultimately it is still the favour of God that brings life. I have known of people who used modern medical technology to help with their conception but it is inevitably fraught with risks and the hazards of failing. It is still the intervening hand of God that brought a prophetic assurance into their hearts that all was well.

Miracles do happen. It is the product of a living faith. The arrival of a child implies a massive journey of life ahead but in the meantime, it is all celebration of a new life.

It is all to the glory of God!

"So many miracles have not yet happened."

Kate DiCamillo, *Flora and Ulysses: The Illuminated
Adventures*

Chapter 7

Something You Have Been Waiting For

My ministry across Australia has taken me to numerous churches and congregations, from the more ethnic ones to those that were largely Caucasian in population. The diversity of population groups within Australian churches are interesting to say the least and it often evokes the question of differences between the sub-groups, both in terms of cultural norms as well as in terms of particular rituals and/or practices.

In some ways, the sub-groups are distinct one to the other. For example, the more ethnic ones generally tend to be more conservative, subdued and traditional whilst the more Australian ones are clearly more vibrant, like the buzz and generally are neither conventional nor restrained. They tend to be more contemporary. Of late, I have been witnessing a blend of the two in what I label as the "new Australian" church, a combination of the better of the two worlds. It is a good development and I thoroughly enjoy ministering in the 'new Australian" congregations.

Yet in many ways, the two groups or indeed the blended groups are not dissimilar one to the other. At the human level, they are absolutely identical. I discovered that people at the core of their needs and existence are on the same platform irrespective of how they perceive each other. When they look for help they all begin from the same starting point.

Hence, the altar ministry in churches levels out every difference between these groupings. Whatever the colour, creed or culture, a sick person is a sick person before God looking for the same mercy and compassion. Notwithstanding the differences and approaches, a person in desperate need for the miraculous is marked not by what divides them but by what is common to them – in their suffering, hope, faith and the desire for healing.

In this atmosphere I lose my ethnicity but I gain my authority and anointing. I minister very effectively to the person at the altar.

My experiences tell me that it is the same tears, the same brokenness, the same desperate cry for help and the similar needs that drive people to God. If a miracle for finances or physical healing is needed, it is the same miracle whatever one's orientation or ethnicity. For this reason, I love to pray for and with people at the altar. Here we are all on common ground. We are equal in our cry for help, equal in our desire for the miraculous and equal in joy and celebration when the inconceivable phenomenon takes place.

In this environment, I find empowerment to engage individuals and to connect them to the Almighty God who alone can give them the supernatural. In this atmosphere I lose my ethnicity but I gain my authority and anointing. I minister very effectively to the person at the altar. I can speak freely, almost uninhabited and sometimes, the eloquence, articulation and insight astounds me for good measure.

I believe it is an atmosphere where our commonality comes to the fore. In this unity, we see and experience comfort, encouragement, strength and the miraculous. In a sense we unlock heaven, no different to what happened in the Old Testament story of the tower of Babel.[46] Scriptures tell us that God observed the people on a common ground, *"people speaking the same language"* and then stating in that environment *"nothing they plan to do will be impossible for them"*.[47]

> *It is the openness of the atmosphere at the altar... It is here that the genesis of a miracle takes place. It is here that the miraculous and the supernatural are birthed.*

From a ministry point of view, the spiritual gifting within my life comes alive at the altar contact. Words, scriptures, impressions, mental images, thoughts, discernment and the word of knowledge – they spill out of my mouth with uncanny accuracy. A common query that I received from people across the globe is "how did you know?" The truth is I do not know. No one told me in advance. Certainly no pastor takes the trouble to prepare me for the altar ministry – none!

It is the openness of the atmosphere at the altar. The Holy Spirit is at work. It is here that the genesis of a miracle takes place. It is here that the miraculous and the supernatural are birthed. I experienced all sorts of happening but one incident stands out from among the rest. This one is unique and interesting because it is not dramatic as such but ordinary, mundane, very much part and parcel of our human existence.

I was ministering at an Australian church in Melbourne on a Sunday morning. The altar was full of people responding to the word of God. The manifest presence of God was pronounced and people were being touched by the divine everywhere.

I started to pray for individuals. The first man I laid my hands on was an individual whom I vividly remember was bald. As soon as I established a contact point on his forehead, words were flowing from my mouth; words that I was sure not only astounded me but him as well. I found myself saying that there was something he had been waiting for and in thirty days, God is going to do an incredible miracle in his life; and that he must be careful to give God the praise and glory. He was in tears and he promptly fell backward.

I prayed for many more that morning but those words for the first man kept coming back to me. It was as if they haunting me. It kept ringing at the back of my mind. The thoughts troubled me for close to a couple of weeks after. I wondered why would I make such a pronouncement. The more I engaged the thought the more I was in fear and trepidation. I was unsettled until I dwelled on these Words at length – *"you speak but it will not be you speaking, but the Spirit of your Father speaking through you"*.[48]

Soon I was moving on and caught up with travelling and ministry. I had disengaged from thinking about the matter. I had entrusted it to the Lord and in due course had forgotten about it altogether. A few weeks later, back home after a ministry trip, I received an email from Sean[49] and this is his story:

Hi Pastor Teo,

Just wanted to encourage you with this testimony.

You came to [my church] not that long ago and you had a word from God over me. What was said is that something we had been waiting for would come to us within 30 days. I was a little scared at this, as we had been praying all year for a car.

God had spoken to us that he was going to provide a good car without us having to put any money towards it. That was in January and we had been without a car that whole time. I have been praying to God the week before you came; know he was going to provide soon but not knowing when. God kept saying, "I want to show you miracles so in faith believe and know I will provide.

We had been up against all oppositions from family asking how it was going to happen, to even Christian friends saying they didn't think it was a good idea and to maybe go out and get a loan. So we went on week after week borrowing cars and having no car.

So when you came, my prayer for that week had been answered, as did many prayers. 30 days. So we waited and waited and in our final week a couple pulled us aside one day and said God had been leading them to give their car away. It was all that we had asked God for. The car has air-conditioning, power steering, air bags, manual and a 6 CD stacker. Above that they paid for Stamp duty and no money was outlaid for this vehicle. They had it serviced and fixed so no problems and they had it detailed. It was purely God.

One thing you said was that, "It will be easy to thank man for this miracle but to give all glory to God." Well ... that's all that we've been doing. The last few months have been transforming for my wife and myself. I have found my passion for writing music and even writing a children's book. God is pulling us out of the wilderness and finally I am feeling like we've made it through.

I have to thank you for each time you've come to [church]. Every time I know you will be uncompromising with the Word of God and tell it like it is. You have inspired me back into ministry as I had been studying at [Bible College] in 2004. I am looking to go back and finish this year. I see the amazing things God is doing for you and I said, "Hey God, you promised me so many good things I'm going to get up, pick up my mat and walk". No longer do I want to walk with burdens on my life. I have a real passion to see the hurting of this nation, from the outback to the cities knowing that there is some purpose in their lives, and that was all from hearing the amazing things that God did through you in Russia.

I pray that things grow and grow for you and Dorothy over this year. God truly has a mighty hand on both your lives.

God Bless
Sean"

Miracles do happen. When you are expecting things to happen, you sow the seeds for the miraculous to come into fruition. You create the genesis to new beginnings. It is the product of a living faith. It was good for Biblical times; it is still good for our contemporary times, even in the mundane things of the modern life!

It is all to the glory of God!

"In thinking about miracles, I believe that our frame of reference has been too dramatic. We have been looking for the burning bush, the parting of the sea, the bellowing voice from heaven. Instead we should be looking at the ordinary day-to-day events in our lives for evidence of the miraculous, maintaining at the same time a scientific orientation."

M. Scott Peck, *The Road Less Traveled: A New Psychology of Love, Traditional Values, and Spiritual Growth*

Chapter 8

Thankful To God That He Made It Possible

Over the last eleven years my ministry has taken me to numerous nations across the globe. However, the bulk of my travelling is within the Asian region and I visited and ministered in one particular nation for countless number of times.

This nation is considered a "closed" country in that it has a near exclusive policy on religious matter. The country does not necessarily welcome Christianity. It continually seeks to limit the influence of the churches within its border, except for the few that are allowed, thanks to its early history. Its policies are often designed to restrict if not remove the Church altogether. Yet this is the nation that I visited repeatedly because its people are open and hungry for the Word.

God's word can never be shut out, no matter how man might try. This has been demonstrated over and over again in history. No empire or generation has succeeded in destroying or shutting out the Christian faith. The Roman Empire failed. The Soviet Union failed. Communist China attempts to destroy the church for years only to discover an underground church of some 155 million people today.[50]

It is the futility of the human mind that seeks to destroy or limit the influence of the church, which by the way is the only organization Jesus gave to the world.[51] The church may be full of flaws, warts and all but this does not detract from the fact that it is God's only institution for the good of the world.

And it is to the church, the communities of believers across the globe that I bring my ministry with the view to empower, encourage and strengthen the body of Christ. Having been to twenty-four countries and more than sixty cities to date, and ministered to a variety of congregations, I must confess that I thoroughly enjoyed interacting with and blessing the people of God.

The church may be full of flaws, warts and all but this does not detract from the fact that it is God's only institution for the good of the world.

There are challenges of course. Not everyone is always accommodating or open to what I have to share. Not everyone concurs with what I say and people do not agree all the time. Often you face and feel rejection and indifference. Yet more often than not, you find people who are great listeners. They listen with attention to learn and appropriate, not to critique or to nit-pick on you.

As a preacher you look forward to your message being well received by your listeners – and better still to hear or obtain positive feedback from them. It is not that you are dependent on these feedbacks to keep you going. It is that often only an email, a phone text, a testimony or a short note of encouragement is sufficient to give you tons of encouragement to persevere and help you keep on with what you have been called to do.

The feedback need not necessarily be about your ministry per se or your sermon points in particular. It could simply be someone resonating with your personal experiences that you are sharing. It may be someone who went through a similar episode in life perhaps went through the same hardship, challenges and the resulting breakthrough. These individuals found encouragement that God has similarly allowed events and the miraculous in your life to mirror what had happened in theirs.

While ministering at a church at the capital city of this particular "closed" nation in December 2005, I met such a person. He was wonderfully touched during the Sunday service. He was so moved that the miraculous I experienced had similarly occurred in his life. In his words, he was actually thinking of not attending church that Sunday morning but was really glad that he did as he was greatly blessed by listening to a similar miraculous happening. It reminded him of the faithfulness of our living God. He was quick to drop me an email to share his story.

Dear Pastor Steven

Greetings in the name on our Lord and Savior Jesus Christ!

Last Sunday I am very thankful to God that He made it possible for me to come to church. That Sunday I was thinking of not attending the service because it was late and I had to do some personal things.

In your sermon, you shared about your wife when she had to go through different tests, procedures and after seven years on then she conceived. Upon hearing your testimony I really wanted to cry ... I wanted to cry because we have the same testimony. Let me share my miraculous story with you.

I grew up in a Christian home and my wife was a Catholic then. We got married in December 1999 and my wife's wedding gift for me was three wonderful words – she said was a "born-again Christian"!

In our marriage we prayed for a baby but nothing happen. We kept praying and at the same time consulted some specialists for help. My wife took some medicines and had some procedures but still did not conceived. My wife got so frustrated that she even stopped praying and asking God for a baby. One of the doctors even told us that my wife has only 25% chances of getting pregnant. I know by faith God will answer our prayers in His time.

In May 2001 when my wife and I decided to go on a mountain climbing trip. That night I causally asked my wife why she did not buy [bring] her napkins along. It then hit us - and we realised that she was one month past her period. We bought a pregnancy test kit and in the early morning of the following day around 1AM we did the test. The test result was positive and both of us were totally surprised. We did not know what to say we just were so excited. We simply thanked God, hugged each other and went back to bed.

In January 29, 2002 at 11PM my wife gave birth to a healthy boy. God blessed us with a very smart child and no one can stop us thanking God for His precious gift of life. Did you know that my son love to sing Christian songs and some of his favorite songs are "Majesty", "Immanuel" and "Awesome God".

Thank you for spending your time reading this e-mail, God bless you and your family and also your ministry.

In Christ,
JIIJ

The miraculous is for every Christian. We must be at home in both the natural and the supernatural worlds. We must be supernaturally natural yet naturally supernatural! We must expect and enjoy spiritual phenomena.

The Apostle James just about proclaimed this fact when he wrote *"Is anyone among you in trouble? Let them pray - Is anyone among you sick? Let them call the elders of the church to pray over them and anoint them with oil in the name of the Lord. And the prayer offered in faith will make the sick person well; the Lord will raise them up - The prayer of a righteous person is powerful and effective.*[52]

I wrote in the earlier chapter that I believe desert phenomena like those experienced by the ancient Israelites are for our contemporary times – and it is often the miraculous within our living faith that attests to the authenticity and truth of the Gospel. Whether it is to bring healing to the sick, peace of mind to the troubled or asking God to bless a marriage with a child, we need to exercise the "prayer of faith" to bring into existence the miraculous.

We must be supernaturally natural yet naturally supernatural!

This is precisely the time for contemporary believers to gear up their spirituality. Our society is not at all unspiritual. David Kinnaman in his book, "*unChristian*" wrote, "Surprisingly, the Christian faith today is perceived as disconnected from the supernatural world – a dimension that the vast majority of outsiders believe can be accessed and influenced."[53] This is a challenge that requires a Christian response to reconnect with the spiritual; not only as a belief system but a conviction that gets a better hold of the individual Christian and collectively the church.

Miracles do happen. I am glad that the gentleman found the courage to share his story. Our faith is indeed a living one; vibrant, authentic, relevant and totally empowering for our earthly existence.

God has a miracle for you because it is all to his glory!

"When others doubt the power of Jesus, be the one who asks Him to perform the impossible. He often will."

Dillon Burroughs, *Thirst No More: A One-Year Devotional Journey*

Chapter 9

God Is Still Working On My Case

In January 2013 I took a team of wonderful people to tour the Holy Land. There I met a team member from Singapore who had such an astonishing story of recovery from a stroke that I had to have her testify of her healing and progress. It was the best story I have heard in a long time.

Her story was simple yet powerful. In fact, so powerful that the guard at the Biblical site attempted to disrupt the sharing by trying to break up our gathering. Due to the rain, we had sheltered at a corner near the entrance and he was determined to undermine us by shifting his furniture for no rhyme or reason. The Israeli guide took me aside and asked if I had noticed the spirituality of this disruption!

Her compelling story is here for you to read.

In May 2000 I remember waking up as I passed motion and realized that I have no strength and no memory. I woke up again when a nurse was cleaning me rather roughly lifting my legs and shoving my body. I cannot and do not even know how to resist. My body felt dead. Then in a wheelchair, I was led to a room for exercise. They tied me to the exercise post, as I could not stand upright. My condition was so bad that I actually fell asleep whilst tied to it.

I woke up with a man next to me claiming to be my husband. He said I had a stroke after delivering our third child. He told me we have three children. He was very nice and took good care of me cleaning me up each time I soiled or spilled food. I disliked the pureed food served by the hospital but could not find proper words to voice my frustration. I have no strength for anything, either to shower or brush my teeth. It felt really cruel having a nurse splashing water over me, drying and clothing me. It felt worse than a baby. I felt terrible and unloved.

During my hospitsalisation, I was allowed to go home once a week. Home then was a three-storey unit. Given my condition, I was on the ground floor all the time. My husband accompanied and slept on the ground floor with me. Two months later, I was discharged from the hospital. In all I was there for a month being in a comatose stage for three weeks.

My husband, children, parents, brother, and mother-in-law came to see me regularly but memory was vague. The funny thing is that I don't remember seeing anyone when hospitalised and only gained memory much later.

My Husband
The truth was that once he really loved and cared for me. I could remember our courtship including when I assisted him to set up his medical practice. Thank God that I kept these wonderful memories. They were not erased by the stroke. It was the everyday memory that I could not remember.

Initially I was left at home when my husband went to work. Those periods of inactivity were unhealthy to say the least. I slept most of the times and was putting on weight. When my husband found out that I was asleep most times, he brought me to his clinic during work.

At the clinic, I sat at the reception counter, packed medicine and did some data input. I had typing skills so keying was not an issue for me. The problem was that I was still talking gibberish and could not comprehend people because my brain was still not connecting. It was such an irony. Where once I was training the staff at the clinic, now they were training me for those simple tasks

I happily followed my husband in and out of the clinic. He acted like my crutch. I was paralysed on my right side and had to hold on to his shoulder to walk. The whole of my right side did not listen to me. I am right handed by birth but I kept using my left hand. It was weird. My husband took care of me for three years.

In a way, it was fun growing up with my children. My mind was that of a child.

During this time, I gained a lot more weight. It was so bad that I was finally given Fenofibrate[54] by my medical doctor husband to address my deteriorating health.

All these while my children were growing by leaps and bounds. I frolicked with them like I was a child. We had so much fun and laughter. Often my mother-in-law, out of frustration having to deal with us would chide me as if I was one of them. She now had to contend not with her three grandchildren but a fourth - me! In a way, it was fun growing up with my children. My mind was that of a child. We would sing and dance around the dining room table. We would play the game of hide and seek. We would play "catching" with me having to catch up with them. Really one big clumsy Mama I was!

Up until now, my husband was apparently loving and caring. He did not grumble or complain. He brought me for trips on a regular basis, sometimes along with his doctor friends. He was helpful even. Meanwhile I was fat and becoming clumsy. I was snacking non-stop. My teeth were getting rotten and in the end had to pull three molars out.

These happy days did not last long. Once my husband was out with his friends and came back very happy. Then he started to tell me that he had many girlfriends out there. I was unfazed not realizing what was happening. He further instructed that I should not assist in the clinic anymore. And when I did turn up for work, he would send me home. The day came when he wanted to introduce his girlfriend requesting that I should be friendly with her. I was still somewhat clueless and followed him along. To my utter shock and surprise she was one of the clinic assistants. She was a much older woman with a husband of her own and two daughters!

She got into the car and sat behind me. We were dropped at the cinema to buy our tickets for the show. I was supposed to purchase three tickets for the three of us. For some reasons, I stopped to tell her to leave my husband alone. She looked surprised and walked away. Before long my mobile phone rang. It was my husband instructing me to return to his car. When I came back I found the woman sitting next to him in the vehicle. I refused to get in until she was out of that front seat!

I was mortified. I kept that word on my mobile phone for two years. I had refused to erase it.

We were driven to a block of flats in the town of Jurong[55]. There we alighted and were sitting with each of us flanking my husband on the side. He then insisted that we holds hands and be sisters. I absolutely refused. However, my feelings were bottled-up and no words came to my mouth. When it was all over, the woman texted me the word, "freak"! I was mortified. I kept that word on my mobile phone for two years. I had refused to erase it. In truth, that word gave me "Frankenstein" energy. Whenever I fell I would look at that word to give me this extra energy. When I looked at that word I felt an energy going through my dead and lifeless body!

My Recovery

By now, I was very determined to get well. I decided that I needed to exercise. I did - three times a day. It was very difficult. Each time I exercised, there was such a pressure to ease myself. As a result I was totally familiar with all the toilets along the West Coast of Singapore![56] Being unable to swim in a straight line, I would walk the treadmill in the morning at the swimming club and again in the afternoon at home. I also walked the estate in the evening. I kept tripping even if the road surface was flat. I would trip on small stones and even leaves! It was as if my feet do not belong to me. I had bruises all over and became insensitive to them. The added pressure of wanting to ease myself kept coming whenever I fell or when I was apparently lost for direction.

In the meantime, I kept praying at a Chinese temple where my husband and I used to frequent until I discovered that he brought the woman there as well. From that point I stopped visiting.

One day when I was exercising, walking as fast as I could, I met a patient from my husband's clinic. She invited me to her church for a miracle service on a particular Saturday. I said I would if I were left alone at home. I was keen to attend as well as I knew that the woman with my husband was attending that church. I wanted to find out what kind of people attends such a church.

Saturday was usually our family day. We would gather as a huge extended family for an outing. All that changed after that fateful day of meeting his girlfriend. From then on, it was a cat and mouse game, with the extended family away on an outing minus me, no matter how hard I tried to be part of the fun! That significant Saturday the same thing happened with my husband picking up everyone except me.

True to my word, I decided to attend the service and took public transport to the meeting. Along the way, the route took me passed the same block of flats at Jurong; immediately anger and pain swelled within my heart. I had to turn my head away from seeing the apartments. At that moment I felt I could chew the woman up for breakfast if I saw her.

I lost my way and had to be directed to the church building. Once there, I stepped into the hall and noticed many friendly faces welcoming me and shaking my hands. I felt loved. No one was shaking my hands for a long time. Stepped into the sanctuary and they were all singing. I felt warmth and a distinctive welcome. The music was also lovely and the preacher was such a fatherly pastor. When the meeting was over, I was invited to join some members for supper. Wow, for once I really felt loved. I had forgotten my first intention of attending that church was to hate the people. Subsequently I joined them every Saturday.

I also attended their cell group meeting and grew from strength to strength. Whilst I did not contribute much to the discussion or the subsequent supper, my mental and spiritual health were improving wonderfully. Indeed, I was looking forward to the Friday night cell meeting.

My strength was such that one day I approached my husband and asked for his credit card to be returned to me. I had given him the card when he was a medical student then. In front of him, I snipped the card with a big pair of scissors but retreated into my room for a good cry! I cried in part because I had forgotten how to sign my name and subsequently had to use fingerprint for transactions instead.

Stepped into the sanctuary and they were all singing. I felt warmth and a distinctive welcome.

My Work
In my fifth year I was approached to help run a pharmaceutical store, working part time but feeling unprepared and inadequate. I had to contend with memory lost and was

struggling to remember things from one end of the store to the other.

Although I was improving hugely my speech was still gibberish and I was forgetful. I had read and decided to join the AKLTG's training seminar[57] to further improve myself. After attending three sessions over three weekends, hearing very impressive speakers who were dynamic and animated, I was extremely fired up to change. I signed up to join a real estate agency, attended their training, did field trips and eventually closed three deals. I finally felt that I could talk!

I was praying God's presence into the workplace, speaking his peace, grace and mercy into my work environment.

My work at the pharmaceutical store came to a stop but was thankfully offered a similar job at a Polyclinic. It was a small miracle as the job had been vacant for six months and no one had applied for it. After I was accepted for the work, six other people were applying for it. The work was difficult and everyday I was praying for help. My problem was not the knowledge of medicine as the stroke did not erased my pharmaceutical memory. It was my everyday memory that was the issue. I had problems using the computing system. Thankfully with the help of others I simply had to focus on dispensing the medicines and throughout the first year my mind really improved. Thank God for people in my cell group who were encouraging and praying for me. I was praying God's presence into the workplace, speaking his peace, grace and mercy into my work environment.

In the meantime, I joined a ministry in praying for sick people at the hospitals. It was most difficult often finding myself not being able to pray. I would open my mouth and no words would come out. My mind would be blank. Others in the ministry were assisting and coaching me and I am thankful to God for these great brethren.

My Weight
I asked God to help me to lose some weight. At first the effort was very successful. I shed 12kg reducing from 72kg to 60kg. However, I was soon stagnant at 60kg. In truth, I was still snacking all the time. I found myself praying that Jesus would teach me to shut my mouth! I determined to eat a full breakfast, skip lunch and have dinner with my children. It didn't work at all. I just kept snacking.

However, after praying for seven years, one day something clicked on the inside. It was a really busy day at work and I had skipped lunch and snacks with no apparent problem. I remember looking at my watch. Hallelujah! It was 5:55pm, five more minutes to six where I could have my dinner! I kept praying and looking at my watch – 5:56pm, 5:57pm, 5:58pm, 5:59pm and finally 6:00pm! Now I could eat and I immediately stuffed bread into my mouth and gobbled it up. I was really so hungry.

That was my first breakthrough with food. However, it is God's word that stirs up the hunger in me now. I have been reading one Christian book per week and the book, "Destined to Reign"[58], especially motivated me. God has woken the sleeping beauty in me!

My Divorce
In 2008 my husband handed me the divorce papers. I ran away from him hoping that he would change his mind. Instead he left the papers on our bed. We had been separated for five years even though we stayed in the same house.

In his affidavit my husband noted that I had a boyfriend. My lawyer refuted that stating that he was the one with a girlfriend. He did not deny the fact. He wanted to have custody of the children as he felt that I was of unsound mind. I agreed for the sake of the children so that they can be together without any separation. He wanted maintenance and support for the children but I was barely able to support myself. I was really sad.

When my son heard the news, he broke down in tears. Soon he was seeing a psychiatrist. I made a resolve then to recover for the sake of my children. Thank God I persisted and now they love me and need not feel forsaken by their mother. They knew I would be there for them. It is mother's love.

For more than a year I stayed with my parents before I bought a place to be within walking distance to my children's home. My in-laws were especially mean, making fun of me with puns and slurring terms. It was just as well that in those years, my head was not connecting and therefore I was above these nasty frays! Today I have forgiven them. I am currently out of my marital home for almost four years.

My children have grown and are now teenagers. They are physically grown but their minds are still young and impressionable. I am praying that I will be the one who will mold them to know Jesus. I am praying that my in-laws will see Christ in me and embrace my simple faith. This is also my prayer for my ex-husband. Things may be changing, where in the past my in-laws were not happy with my visiting the children, they are now welcoming me. They can see my love for them.

> In truth, Jesus comes to heal and to bless. We only have to believe.

I thank God that I am being healed and sharing the Good news whenever possible. In truth, Jesus comes to heal and to bless. We only have to believe.

My Trip To Israel
A cell member invited me to attend a talk by a pastor about visiting Israel. And so in September 2010 I stepped onto the Holy Land. I remember running into the State and kissing the ground. I felt so blessed that I was finally in the land! I had no expectation but felt that God had led me there for a purpose.

I had a great time in the land – listening to sermons and enjoying the Dead Sea. I was able to touch the mud and walked the viscous seawater. Only when I came back to Singapore did I realise what God had done. He had woken me. I have been sleeping all these while. Since my stroke I always felt as if my body was here on this earth but I was missing. My spirit man within me was awakening. Following the trip I found myself very alert and alive.

My spirit man within me was awakening. Following the trip I found myself very alert and alive.

I did my second trip to Israel in September 2011 following a couple of great leaders from Singapore.[59] Upon returning I discovered God had blessed me with feelings and intuition.

My third trip to Israel was in January 2013. This time round there were six pastors in the group. We had such wonderful fellowship and speaking God's word at every significant Biblical site. Different pastors were sharing God's word relevant to the particular place. At the Pool of Bethesda, I was called upon by Pastor Steven to share my healing and recovery story. I had such fun. This time round, God had indeed blessed me with humour and laughter

Continuing Recovery
I am thankful for those who assisted and encouraged me in my difficult journey. In particular I am grateful for Baby Goh who literally walked me to my health. I remember the times she invited

me to walk with her along the canal next to her home. She would pray with me and held on to me because I leaned towards my right. She taught me Bible verses and shared God's love with me.

She told me to forgive my ex-husband which was a challenging thing to do. God spoke to me one day to do just that. I also erased the "freak" word from my mobile phone. It was another miracle and clearly a milestone in my continuing journey of life.

God willing I will be making my fourth trip to the Holy Land. I believe that God will progress my healing to its completion. I believe for complete and total healing such that there should be no more numbness on my right side. God is still working on my case.

My sister's story is faith building. At the time of writing this book, she had visited and encouraged my friend's wife who also suffered a stroke. A massive surgery had taken place and his wife is now recovering in a local hospital in Singapore, awaiting an ongoing rehabilitation program. The visit was awe-inspiring and was such an encouragement to my friend and family. I was told his wife was thoroughly inspired by this life and this story! She too is now on the road to recovery!

Miracles do happen.

"Miracles are like meatballs, because nobody can exactly agree what they are made of, where they came from, or how often they should appear."

Lemony Snicket

Chapter 10

The Best Coffin Was My Last Gift

I was in-between finishing Law School and commencing my legal practical training and internship in the middle of 2013. There was a small window of opportunity for me to travel and minister, something I love to do and has been doing for the last eleven years since I left the corporate world for the ministry. The last three years of Law School had been utterly demanding of my time and energy. I was glad that the discipline was over and I could now look forward to travelling again.

I felt that I should be ministering in the northern part of West Malaysia, so I contacted a good friend in Penang to arrange and schedule the itinerary. Part of the journey took me to a church in the town of Kulim, Kedah.[60] We had a special meeting on the Saturday night. The Word was preached and it ministered to many in the congregation.

When the meeting was over, the pastors together with my visiting friends took me out for supper. This is very typical of Malaysian hospitality. Wonderful fellowship over an excellent meal is imperative for the longevity of any ministry!

It was during this fellowship that Vijay Abel, wife of the senior pastor of the church, Paul Abel, told her life story of how God took her from death, healed her and released her into her destiny. Her story was enthralling. There she was, having a great meal with us, telling us that she was given up for dead and that she should not have been alive. Yet an hour ago, she was worship leading the church; passionate, vibrant, full of buzz and totally lost in the worship of the Almighty God. She also told us about her frequent ministry trips to Cambodia and Vietnam; how she is probably more recognisable there in those nations than in her own country. She is feeding the poor, caring for the uncared and bringing the Gospel of good news to the Cambodians and Vietnamese.

She is truly a walking miracle, sitting right there, having a drink and a meal with us, chatting away, laughing and having fun ...

I was really excited. I told Vijay that I was writing a book on the living faith; that miracles do happen. I suggested that her story, the fact that she is truly a walking miracle; sitting right there, having a drink and a meal with us, chatting away, laughing and having fun, should be told so that readers around the globe would be blessed, inspired and standing in awe of the living God because of her phenomenal testimony.

What a thrill it was when I received Vijay's email detailing her story. Here is her story:

At the age of eleven I participated in a school walkathon. I completed the five miles stride but finally collapsed after finishing the event. All I knew was that I landed in the hospital. The doctors diagnosed my situation and suggested that I had a weak heart.

Following that episode, I was frequently breathless and feeling very exhausted all the time. I was put on all sorts of medication, consuming up to four or five different kinds of medicine at any one time. All along the way my condition was deteriorating. My health was increasingly getting worse.

I was soon back to a private hospital in Penang where the doctors did a scan and discovered that I had a hole in my heart. This was the reason for my continual breathlessness, feeling tired all the time and generally being lethargic. With that diagnosis, the doctors added more medication for my consumption. More medical tablets were added to treat me after each finding.

I am the only daughter of a single mother. I lived with my grandparents who were originally from India. They were my caregivers and took care of me in my growing years. My grandparents were strong believers in Hinduism. Seeing my suffering they took me to different temples, seeking a cure for me. They were deeply concerned for my well being. They were desperate enough for my health such that though they were Hindus, they willingly took me to Chinese temples as well, all the time seeking for my healing.

The continuing deterioration of my health took a toll on me. I was soon into depression. Fear took a better grip of me. There was much pain in my little existence. I was constantly in and out of hospital. The many trips to the hospital for check-up and/or treatment made me sicker. My mother could not take the pain and burden anymore. She has had enough of the suffering. Even my grandparents were badly discouraged and disheartened.

By now I was twenty years of age. I was absolutely weak and sickly. The sickness was a huge burden on me. I was on the edge. I was giving up on life. I had no more strength left, if you will.

Finally, even the doctors gave up on me. They discharged me from the hospital and told my family to take me home. They suggested that my end was nearing; that death would inevitably come. They further suggested that my family call all their friends and relatives to pay me their final visits, as death would be the natural outcome of my situation. By then, my medical condition was really bad. I was turning colour all the time. It was as if the texture of my skin

76

was frequently changing colour. It was blue on and off indicating that my days would soon be over.

My grandfather was heart-broken but in true tradition of a Hindu man, he had my good in mind. He was preparing the best coffin as the last gift for me. If I had to go, then I would have to go knowing that he cared for me!

During that time, there was a young girl who used to park her bicycle at our house on her way to school. She was also a young Christian but obviously one who knows her living faith in her God. She asked my grandfather for permission to pray for me, "Can I pray for her?" I want you to know that because we were staunch Hindus, a belief in Jesus Christ or the practice of Christianity was never allowed in our home. It was not something we could seriously engage in among our generations within the household.

I found myself murmuring the words she has spoken. I was regurgitating her prayers.

Notwithstanding that, my grandfather was surprisingly open about it. The years of heartache and despair must have taken a toll on his belief system. He was desperate for anything that could help his granddaughter. His response to the young Spirit-filled Christian schoolgirl, who was only fifteen years of age, was amazing. He said to her, "We have done all we can for our granddaughter, you can do yours."

I remember my eyes were closed and I was breathing heavily. Suddenly there was a soft whisper in my ears. I grasped the words that said, "Jesus heal me". Next day the young girl came by again. This time, she prayed, "By the stripes of Jesus I am healed".[61] On the third day, all I heard were these words, "The blood of Jesus".

She kept coming by and praying. This went on for two weeks. I found myself murmuring the words she has spoken. I was regurgitating her prayers. I had heard about Jesus in Sunday school but this was different. I soon felt totally different. Something was flowing through my body that I could not explain till this day. The young girl's prayers brought life into my otherwise dying body. Suddenly my health was improving by leaps and bounds.

I wisely continued my medication but my supply of medicine was exhausted after two months. Quite naturally, I sought for more medication. Soon, I was going back to the doctors for more medicine without prior medical appointment. However, this time my trips to the doctors were vastly different. I was not being carried into the clinic or hospital. I was walking into the hospital unaided, all by myself. I had recovered so much that my strength were coming back to me.

The doctors took me to scanning theater to rescan my heart. It took a long time for the results to be made known to me. I waited for forty-five minutes for the doctors to come to a conclusion. I could see a level of commotion. The medical team was toing and froing; they were in and out of the scan theater as if something were amiss.

When God healed me, he does not need surgery! He did it miraculously. It was supernatural and a great phenomenal indeed!

They kept looking at my face and reverting to the patient's card and all the documented films and materials. They had the expression of surprise as if they were looking at either the wrong patient or the wrong set of medical records. Maybe there was an error here, a mixed up and that I was the wrong patient! I told the doctors what had happened; that I was prayed for and that I was now recovering.

The clinical findings are that the hole in my heart had closed as though it was stitched. When God healed me, he does not need surgery! He did it miraculously. It was supernatural and a great phenomenon indeed! All my medications were stopped at once. Jesus came right into my life and healed me.

I subsequently met my husband in his church where he was pastoring, married him and together we now serve the Lord. We are pastoring a church in Kulim but I am also in my own right, a missionary to the nations. I preach, heal and bring deliverance wherever I go, but especially to the poor people in Cambodia, and Indonesia.

My faith is a living one. Miracles do happen – and for me it is a life-long testimony of the mercy and graciousness of our Lord Jesus Christ.

All glory to the living God!"

"Sometimes we get caught up in trying to glorify God by praising what He can do and we lose sight of the practical point of what He actually does do."

Dallas Willard

Chapter 11

Completely Healed of Prostate Cancer!

I first met Jim in 2004 when I was ministering in Perth, Western Australia. I was there ministering through a Singapore church connection. The ministry was good and soon I was preparing to return to Melbourne. In a short discussion with the pastor I was asked if I would meet a minister who is regarded as the "father of FGA churches" in Perth.[62] This was Jim's mentor and the senior minister of his church.

He had heard about my ministry and extended an invitation for me to meet up with him and his leadership team. It was in that meeting that I first saw Jim and over the years, relishes the growth of our relationship. It was divine appointment indeed. God certainly put two people together for good reasons. Since then, Jim has been a good friend, supporter, fellow minister and my *InSight*[63] member for as many years as I can remember!

Jim is a practicing accountant and he has his own practice in Perth. But it was more than just a profession or a business. By all account he is pastoring Hay Street in Subiaco, the west of Perth! I remember occasions when I visited him in his office, only to be marched down the street into praying for a few businesses and individuals. I can remember individuals calling him "Pastor Jim" as we walked the street!

His office holds a once-a-week meeting for people in the marketplace. This is the place people gather regularly and individuals are prayed for in their situations while many others prayed the prayer of salvation in receiving Jesus as Lord and Saviour.

Today Jim ministers in his own right through his own ministry incorporated. He preaches regularly. He also travels and ministers in different nations including Indonesia, Malaysia and Singapore. In April 2012, Jim was in a ministry with me to Nepal. This was a pivotal point of his ministry. I saw him ministering at his best. The prophetic anointing was clearly on his life and he was simply an awesome blessing to the School of Ministry and the churches in Banepa, a city forty-five minutes outside the Kathmandu Valley.

I was in total shock. "How could this be? "I asked myself repeatedly.

In one of my numerous visits to the city, Jim asked me to pray for him and his health. He told of a recent diagnosis of prostate cancer by his doctors. Concern was written all over Jim's face and he was obviously weighted down by this prognosis. It wasn't long before I communicated with Jim again and he wonderfully told me of his encounter with the Lord, and how God was telling him that he was healed of his prostate. A subsequent check-up with the specialist proved him correct and today he is free of the disease.

Here's is Jim's story of how he was completely healed of prostate cancer:

In June 2010, I got the most horrific news from my urologist that I had prostate cancer. The prognosis came after a recent biopsy. I was in total shock. "How could this be? "I asked myself repeatedly.

I am reasonably fit and healthy. I exercises and dances at least four times per week. My wife makes sure that I have a healthy and balanced diet.

Once this nasty piece of news was released to my family members, unrest was stirred within the household. My brother, who resides in Kuala Lumpur, Malaysia, suggested that I undergo an immediate surgery in Singapore from a respected well-known surgeon in this field. Thankfully, I did not do so!

Instead, I went for a second opinion from another urologist and he conducted another biopsy two months later. Then the miracle took place. Right after this second biopsy, I urinated some green substance the very next morning. I somehow knew right in my spirit that ALL the cancer cells in my prostate gland had been discharged. When the result of the second biopsy came there was no further evidence of prostate cancer although the urologist believed there were traces of cancer cells in the prostate gland. Hence, I continue to see the urologist and have blood sample taken for my prostate condition once every six months. In one of my blood test, the reading of PSA level increased from over 6 to 9.69. This was in September 2011.

I somehow knew right in my spirit that ALL the cancer cells in my prostate gland had been discharged.

During this period, I visited the toilet almost hourly. It was tough and hard going. The situation appears to be not so positive. My urologist suggested surgery to widen my urinal as my prostate was very enlarged and it was putting extreme pressure on my urinal. I told my urologist to give me three months to consider the matter. In that time, I prayed and seek God over the decision.

I was convicted by the Holy Spirit to fast during the month of April 2012 even though I was on a mission trip to Nepal during that season. During my whole trip in Nepal I fasted and only started eating after lunchtime each day. The team was enjoying their food whilst I was abstaining from it even though I was with them at all meals. Nepali food was surprisingly tasty and good. Members of the team were fully aware of my fast and a couple were teasing me on how awesome the food was!

After my return from Nepal, I did another blood test on the 1st of May and on the 3rd May 2012 I had an appointment to see my urologist. The result of the test showed a huge decrease in the PSA reading. It went from 9.69 to 3.64. The urologist announced to me that I did not require surgery to widen my urinal as the prostate enlargement had shrunk to the normal size. Praise the LORD I am back to the usual!

To monitor the condition of my prostate situation, I continue to see my urologist once every six months. In February 2013, after two and three-quarter years of the first prognosis, I was asked to do another biopsy on my prostate situation. This time the result showed no evidence of any cancer in my prostate gland. Hallelujah! I am totally healed of prostate cancer.

My healing comes because I totally believe that my Lord Jesus has already healed all my diseases on the cross more than two thousand years ago. There is healing in the atonement. There is healing at the foot of the cross. I partake the Holy Communion very regularly in memory of what Jesus did for me that day. Jesus instituted this sacrament. He mandated that we remember precisely because there is power in remembering His death.

> There is healing in the atonement. There is healing at the foot of the cross.

He said, "Do this, in remembrance of me."[64] This memory has special meaning – when we remember something from the past, we do not merely entertain a pale idea of it; we actually make it present again, make it once more potent in our lives! This act of memory makes us partakers of His body and blood, of Jesus Christ's death and passion. We appropriate God's completed work into our existence. We make alive his act of unfailing and unconditional love.

The act of partaking in the Holy Communion is very powerful as embedded in this sacrament is our healing and deliverance, not only for our bodies but our spirits and souls. In appropriating this memory, all of my sicknesses had already been nailed on the cross and Jesus' blood cleanses me of all my unrighteousness. I had a complete medical check-up recently and my doctor's comment was my whole body was like that of "a young man". This reminds me of what the Psalmist said, " [God] who satisfies your desires with good things so that your youth is renewed like the eagle's."[65] Praise God!

I somehow knew right in my spirit that ALL the cancer cells in my prostate gland had been discharged.

My current PSA reading is 2.05 which is normal for the prostate gland. At the time of writing this story I am sixty-six years old and still running my own accounting practice in Perth. I am more energetic than before. Besides running an accounting practice, I am also an elder of a church. I am actively serving the Lord in the marketplace in Perth and beyond.

The Lord is so gracious and merciful to me that HE not only healed me on my prostate cancer but I am also amazingly healed of eczema, diabetes, high blood pressure, high cholesterol and dandruff. I no longer need to wear spectacles which I wore for *over fifty years. My optician told me to throw my spectacles away. I guess these are stories for another book!*

Praise the Lord! All the Glory goes to my Lord Jesus!

Jim is a living testimony of God's miraculous and the supernatural. He is a walking miracle and this is evidenced by the fact that wherever he goes, individuals who encountered him are being led to the Lord Jesus.

Miracles do happen.

"To live at all is miracle enough."

Mervyn Peake, *Collected Poems*

Chapter 12

The Spectacular Or The Supernatural

Our society is generally consumed with the spectacular. It is an embedded part of the celebrity culture. This culture worships the accomplished, the grand and the magnificent. It is performance based and implicitly seeks for perfection. It is a humanistic belief system that has insidiously crept into our Christian belief system.

Hence part of being a contemporary church is to assume a level of perfection. We settle for only the best, not that the best is wrong but our approach calls for the best, nothing but the best. It is no longer giving it our best because our best may not be enough for many churches seeking to employ or engage individuals in ministry or service. We have appropriated the culture of perfection and with it we continually seek for the showy and the lavish performance.

> *We have appropriated the culture of perfection and with it we continually seek for the showy and the lavish performance.*

Unfortunately we also import this behavior into our view of the supernatural. It is therefore not uncommon for many to seek the spectacular in the miraculous. There is an assumption that all miracles are incredibly spectacular; so we chase after instantaneous healing, immediate deliverance and a dramatic if not an almost magical approach to the supernatural.

M. Scott Peck said, "In thinking about miracles, I believe that our frame of reference has been too dramatic. We have been looking for the burning bush, the parting of the sea, the bellowing voice from heaven. Instead we should be looking at the ordinary day-to-day events in our lives for evidence of the miraculous." [66]

I believe God wants to bring the realm of the supernatural into our every day existence, not limited by any of our cultural preferences. Start by discovering the joy of being thrilled with the "small miracles", those that exists in the routines of our lives. They may not be spectacular but they are frequently supernatural. The shift in focus will change your perspective and lead you on the road to a miracle-filled life.

A supernatural may indeed be spectacular but the spectacular may not necessarily be supernatural.

Most people are more comfy with the spectacular whereas God wants us to be comfortable with the supernatural. The two are miles apart both in definition and dynamics. Spectacular is associated with being impressive or attractive whereas supernatural is defined as the miraculous and/or beyond the powers or the laws of nature.[67]

To illustrate this point it would be absolutely true to say that when Lionel Messi[68] scores the kind of goals he does when he plays the game of soccer, it is indeed spectacular. If I were to do that, it is called supernatural. Another example of the distinction between the two is to say that for a thirty-year old man to become a father is spectacular but for Abraham (of the Old Testament story)[69] becoming a father at the age of a 100 years old is supernatural.

A supernatural may indeed be spectacular but the spectacular may not necessarily be supernatural. We miss the cue here and that may explain why as a generation we have lost the thrill of signs and wonders. Ravi Zacharias suggested in his book, *"Recapture the Wonder"* that "there is wonder all around us, and it is God's will to fill us with that wonder that makes life enchanting and sacred."[70] This signs and wonders should not be as elusive as it appears.

Looking for the Spectacular

Our culture seeks the spectacular. For example, we not only want to be successful but visibly so. We have a penchant to display our talent, wealth, accomplishment and experience. People who succeed somewhat in life demonstrate their success in very tangible ways; moving to a better home, drive a better car, have a better holiday, attend a better school, and even being part of a better church.

It is natural to gravitate towards the stunning or outstanding which is why the grand and magnificent is so much part of our fabric. Whether it is in good or bad times, we are more readily convinced if the event is remarkable or impressive. It was no different for people during Biblical times.

> *"There is wonder all around us, and it is God's will to fill us with that wonder that makes life enchanting and sacred"*
>
> *- Ravi Zacharias*

The Gospel of Matthew described the scene where Jesus was being crucified. While he was nailed to the cross, the people who gathered or were passing by hurled insults at him, shaking their heads and suggesting that, *"You who are going to destroy the temple and build it in three days, save yourself! Come down from the cross, if you are the Son of God!"*[71] If indeed Jesus had exercised his divine authority and stepped down from the cross, it would have satisfied the crowd. It would have been been awesomely spectacular. Most certainly it would delight the crowd because they were looking to be impressed.

History tells us that the temple was indeed destroyed by the Roman Army in 70 AD.[72] It was not rebuilt in three days. The second temple may have been rebuilt for more than forty-six years.[73] It had already been that long in the rebuilding process when Jesus ministered there.[74] But Jesus was not tuned into or the least interested in the spectacular, in satisfying the need for a convincing proof or to make an impression on the people. He was talking about the supernatural. He was speaking of his body, which God would raise in three days.

For Jesus the supernatural is for him to stay on the cross. It was the only way to complete God's salvation plan for mankind.

The danger for many of us, living in our pressured-filled, stressed-up contemporary environment, looking for the good temporal life, is that we can miss the supernatural by focusing on the spectacular. We can be caught up with the immediate need for a convincing impression failing which we do not respond. This mindset has an adverse effect on our general expectation of the miraculous. We are boxed-in. We are then poorly positioned for the God experiences in our life which may be happening more in the day-to-day events.

We may seek the spectacular unconsciously. In our sickness, we may seek instantaneous healing – we want it now, matter of fact yesterday! We seek instant cures and instant responses from God. Our prayers can be amazingly self-centered and self-focused. We look for the extraordinary much like the people at the crucifixion situation who missed the whole point altogether. They failed to understand the supernatural because they had the wrong focus. They understood wrongly. They were looking for the wrong thing. God was looking for their hearts but they were looking for their spoils.

You see for Jesus the supernatural is for him to stay on the cross. It was the only way to complete God's salvation plan for mankind. Redemption was purchased. The spectacular would be to step down from the cross but redemption would have been lost –forever.

Looking for the Supernatural

The subsequent resurrection of Jesus following his death and burial was indeed extremely spectacular. It is the only logical conclusion to draw as the Roman guards were in fear and trepidation arising from the event. They were frozen stiff. *"They were so afraid of him [whose appearance was like lightning, and his clothes were white as snow] that they shook and became like dead men"*.[75]

The resurrection is the supernatural power in God's redemption story.

The resurrection may be stunning and out of this world but it is the supernatural power within the resurrection that is truly awesome. God is not interested in the hype-up event per se. He is interested in the continuing ongoing power of the resurrection; the power to heal, to set free, liberate, to save people from the clutches of the evil one, to restore and to affirm – that is what the event was about, though undoubtedly impressive. The resurrection is the supernatural power in God's redemption story.

The power of the resurrection today is in the transformed lives and changed destinies. Mankind now has a means to salvation and a life of purpose and destiny. There is now a way for God to reconcile and reconnect with human kind. This is the supernatural that we can fellowship with God as Jesus Christ has given us right standing with him. It is our heritage. It is meant for us to enhance our existence and to see God at work in every detail of our lives.

Part of being supernatural is an embedded willingness for the miraculous. Therefore have an expectation for a miracle – whatever it is you are looking for, even if it is routine and mundane, sort of a day-to-day occurrence. Put aside all your cultural inhibitions. Cast away all your pre-conceived notions. It does not need to be stunning or impressive.

Is life hard on you? Are events working against you? Are people are turning on you? Well, refocus your sight on the supernatural. The resurrection power of Jesus allows us to look for the supernatural. Let the power of the resurrection course through your existence.

Changing Frame of Reference

A belief in God is a belief in the miraculous as God's dealing and interaction with human kinds is premised on the supernatural. This is implicitly declared in the Old Testament book of Isaiah where the prophet declared that God's *"thoughts are not your thoughts, neither are your ways [his] ways, as the heavens are higher than the earth, so are [his] ways higher than your ways and [his] thoughts than your thoughts".*[76]

In my experience, God's ways are inevitably up side down. They often appear unassuming, unpretentious, illogical,

Therefore have an expectation for a miracle – whatever it is you are looking for, even if it is routine and mundane, sort of a day-to-day occurrence.

irrational and even uneconomical but in it you will discover the miraculous. If you want to see the supernatural, you obviously need to see beyond what is natural to you.

There is an interesting Gospel story mentioned only in the book of Mark. This story is not found in the other three Gospels. This is the passage. *"They came to Bethsaida, and some people brought a blind man and begged Jesus to touch him. He took the blind man by hand and led him outside the village. When he had spit on the man's eyes and put his hands on him, Jesus asked, "Do you see anything?" He looked up and said, "I see people; they look like trees walking around." Once more Jesus put his hands on the man's eyes. Then his eyes were opened, his sight was restored, and he saw everything clearly."*[77]

God wants us to be a people who are supernaturally natural and naturally supernatural.

Not only is this story set apart, it is also unique. It testifies to common sense[78] and shows the Gospel writer's disposition in being as much taken up with the healing, as he was with the way the healing was done. He was dealing with the ordinary, the mundane and the routine in life.

Firstly, the healing was done in two stages. This implies a process could be involved. It need not be spontaneous or spectacular. Secondly, the healing was done differently to many other occurrences. This implies that the approach was unique. God always has a unique place for each individual. He is a personable God, relating with each of us individually, personally, one at a time. Finally, the healing gets better with time. A little delay is not an issue then. This implies that it is okay to keep trying and that continuous improvement in a situation is entirely acceptable.

My point is this: the underlying thrust of God's redemptive healing taking place is never distracted but the approach reveals astonishing insights. I drew a few inferences from this:

a. God is a God of variety.
b. God is a God of diversity.
c. God is a God of uniqueness.
d. God has a different stroke for different people.
e. God is concerned with the routines of our existence.
f. God is indifferent to the spectacular.

God wants us to be a people who are supernaturally natural and naturally supernatural.

And all that does not take the supernatural out of the story. God was in the midst of it. It is his story albeit less impressive and spectacular by human standards.

Truth is, God wants us to be a people who are supernaturally natural and naturally supernatural. He wants us to be a people who walk and live comfortably by revelation and by wisdom.[79] He wants us to be a people whose disposition is conducive to the miraculous intervening hand of an invisible God. We should be at home with the supernatural.

The spectacular may make you sit up but the supernatural will make you sit right. The key is to allow the power of the resurrection to course through your life and begin to walk naturally in the miraculous.

"Most people weren't wired to see miracles, even when one was staring them in the face."

Greg Mitchell

Chapter 13

Seeing The Supernatural

At one point, I had been itinerating for the over two years following my graduation from Bible College. This was a faith ministry in that I received no wage and I was not financially supported by any church or organization. Matter of fact, the ministry is still self-funding and it largely depends on gifts from individuals and honorarium from churches or groups where I minister.

Money was tight. There were no frills. In this environment I was travelling and inevitably you do need to pick up some of the expenses which the ministry was unable to support. This particular trip required a little more than a $1,000 and I had to dip into my own pockets to fund the journey. I wrote the cheque to the travel agent who did the ticketing. While writing the payment, I remember praying a "prayer-wish" – this is a prayer but more a wish. I said, "Lord, it would be nice if someone picks this bill up." It was not really a serious prayer request, more a silent whisper from the heart. I then moved on and promptly forgotten about the event.

While itinerating, I received a phone call from my wife, Dorothy. She told me of a friend calling on the house phone asking for me. When told that her husband was travelling, the caller said that he would call again when I return. As soon as Dorothy hanged the phone, it rang again. It was the same caller. He then asked if she was home and indicated that he would like to visit her straight away as he had a gift to pass on to me. Soon the doorbell rang and he handed an envelope to Dorothy. In it was cash of $996. The caller said it was for my ministry. When I heard the story, I was celebrating. I said Lord, "I am happy to pay a few dollars each time for every one of my ministry trips!"

It was a lesson learnt. Never box God in. The supernatural belongs to the realm of the unexpected. Since then, some of the most wonderful answers to my prayers come from the least expected individuals and/or sources. God continually confounds me with surprises.

In seeing the supernatural, we frequently adopt a habit of boxing God in. We stereotype him and anticipate that there is a certain way he is going to act. In our hearts and minds, we lay an expectation as to how our needs are going to be met and how our prayers are to be answered. Instead of allowing God to own and work the process we maintain an "imposition" and expect tailored processes appropriate to our notion of performance.

Unexpected Source

The supernatural belongs to the realm of the unexpected.

One of the best stories illustrating this point is found in the Old Testament book of 1 Kings chapter 17.[80] In this passage of scriptures, we read of God doing great miracles for the widow at Zarephath. Yet the actual situation for this widow was really challenging. This woman was preparing for the inevitable death by starvation. She and her son would soon have their last meal and that would be the end for the family.

When asked to feed the prophet, she said, "*I don't have any bread – only a handful of flour in a jar and a little oil in a jug. I am gathering a few sticks to take home and make a meal for myself and my son that we may eat it – and die."*[81]

The situation was very critical. It was a desperate and exasperating circumstance. Death would have been everywhere because the land had a severe famine. Yet God had a different idea. He had a different understanding. He was on another dimension altogether. It is apparent that God was not looking at the obvious.

It is apparent that God was not looking at the obvious.

In an earlier passage, God told the Prophet Elijah that he had *"commanded a widow"* to feed him. The significant word here is *"commanded"* – God was orchestrating behind the scene. He did not ask the widow for her permission. The widow did not even know it. She certainly would not have felt like it! She was by all account totally unaware of God's command to feed the prophet with the paltry meal that she was left with. Fact is this was a woman who had almost no means to provide for herself and her son, let alone someone else. This was an unexpected source both to the provider and the receiver.

Nevertheless the widow responded positively. She fetched water for the prophet. She baked and fed the prophet first with her last meal. She gave all that she had to live on and the result was exponential.

Supernatural And The Exponential

The widow not only fed the prophet, she fed herself and her family. Now that is interesting. First the scriptures say she wanted to bake the cake for herself and her son. The picture is a narrow one. It was about personal survival. Next the scriptures talked about the availability of food for her and her family. *"So there was food every day for Elijah and for the woman and her family."*[82] This is talking about an extended family.

When the Old Testament speaks of "family" it has the definition of an enlarged Hebrew family. It means an extended number of people related to the person. It would have naturally included her parents, siblings and their families, uncles, aunties and even distant relatives who may be part of the family or tribe.[83]

Her response in feeding the prophet resulted in her not only being able to supply her own needs (she and her son) but also reaching out to everyone within the extended family structure. In times of famine and great devastation, she was able to feed a large number of people related to her. The supernatural is always associated with the exponential. Outcomes following divine intervention have a tendency to be exceptional. Often God is not interested in anything that stops with the individual. He goes beyond one person. God clearly wanted to bless the widow but he did it his way. In the process, there is a multiplier effect. It appears then that the only blessings you could keep are truly the ones you are willing to give. This runs counter culture to our nature and the culture of our society today.

The supernatural is always associated with the exponential.

I said earlier in the book that we agonize through the twists and turns of our lives without realizing or realize too slow that God owns the process. The supernatural is part of that process. God is not super spiritual but he is a supernatural God who will work behind the scene to demonstrate his love and faithfulness in helping us.

Looking Beyond The Natural

Now this statement seems pretty obvious isn't it? Yet many people want to see the supernatural but could not let go of the natural. They are earthbound. They are rational, logical, economical and more often than not temporal rather than eternal in their thinking. Society has conditioned us so well that anything out of the ordinary or rational is not possible. It is irreconcilable therefore it is impossible. So we add our own sad conclusion to many of our situations by the thoughts, words and actions we apply to the challenges because we deem it impossible. We believe what we see, feel and perceive instead of believing the word of God or what God has to say. We trust the natural instead of stepping out in faith to hold on to the supernatural.

Faith, the raw trust in a living God is the basic ingredient for the supernatural.

The prophet must have looked pretty ordinary to the widow yet he was God's supernatural answer to her need and continued existence. She became part of the supernatural at a time when she least expected it. I am glad that in her arduous times, the widow was not relying on her own feelings or what was rational to her. If she had, she would have missed the opportunity to see and participate in the supernatural.

Initially rational in her approach when asked by the prophet for help, the widow subsequently stepped out in faith. She made the provision against her better judgment. Faith, the raw trust in a living God is the basic ingredient for the supernatural. Jesus in the Gospel of Mark said, " *When you pray, believe that you receive and you will have it.*"[84] Until we wrap our requests in faith and expectation we will get nowhere. God does not respond to our situation per se, he responds to our faith.

101

Scripture says, " *Faith ... is the evidence of things not seen.*" [85]Another translation brings out the central thought of the verse better, "*Faith perceiving as reality those things that are not revealed to the natural senses.*"[86] If we want to see the supernatural, we need to see beyond the natural. We need to see the unseen. Remember, you need faith for what you cannot see, not for what you can see.

A critical aspect of looking beyond the natural lies in our knack to appropriate the mind of Christ, firstly to see the heart of the Father[87] and secondly to see the treasures he has in store for us.[88] If our worldview is filtered through the heart of God, the supernatural will be an expected part of our landscape.

Stretching For The Supernatural

The prophet asked the widow to make him a small cake of bread even though she had barely enough for herself. It stretched her to do this. It was not easy. She did not simply agreed. The prophet had to encourage and assure her. He said, "*Do not be afraid*" implying that there was fear and apprehension. It took courage for the widow to stretch her faith. Courage is never the absence of fear but the mastery of fear.[89]

God wants to continually stretch our faith for the supernatural. He wants us to stretch beyond our comfort zone so that we grow in our understanding of and relationship with him. God does not want us to be just faithful, he wants us to be fruitful, abounding in spirituality and enjoying the supernatural. We can begin to see the invisible hand of God only if we are willing to be stretched.

We can only experience the exploits of the Almighty when we expect and stretch for it.

The Apostle Paul in the New Testament was

stretched to a point of depression. He experienced such hardship in his ministry that at one point he was despairing even of life. In other words, he was stretched to a point of being suicidal. *"We were under great pressure, far beyond our ability to endure, so that we despaired even of life. Indeed in our hearts we felt the sentence of death."*[90] But through his being stretched, this man saw and experienced more of the supernatural than any others.

Staying in the safe and comfort zones of our lives will not trigger the release of the supernatural. Simply wishing for it to happen is not the answer either. We can only experience the exploits of the Almighty when we expect and stretch for it. Often others appear to be experiencing miracles for which we desire ourselves. The crucial factor may be that they stretched for it while we opted for the path of least resistance.

Always About The Impossible

One of the essentials about the supernatural is that we must not fear disappointment or failure.

In the story, God did the impossible by causing the flour to never run out and the oil to never run dry. This was impossibility. The supernatural is always about the impossible.

I wrote about the importance of seeing in chapter two. It is imperative for us to understand that the biblical concept of "seeing" relates to the realm of impossibility. It is something you cannot see ever happening because of the impossibility of it. Your life's experience tells you that it will not happen. Your knowledge tells you that it cannot possibly happen and the facts tell you that it never will happen. Yet faith tells you that it can be reality. It can happen. Against all odds you can see it happening.

Sometimes our challenges are so impossible, we dare not even hope. We do not want our expectation to be dashed. So we do not hope or imagine the impossible ever happening. But it is in the seemingly impossible situations of our life that we are likely to see and experience the miraculous.

One of the essentials about the supernatural is that we must not fear disappointment or failure. We all fail at something every day or are disappointed at one time or another. The only people who do not experience failure or disappointment are the ones who never try. Step out in faith knowing that a miracle can only happen when the situation is impossible, and if not, there is nothing to lose anyway.

Do not be so afraid of failing that you "tiptoe" safely to the grave, without blowing it somewhere along the way! Life is for the living, not simply to exist. Do not waste your days trying to prolong a difficult life. Use every moment of it to ensure a life of exploits and destiny. Go for it. You would have successfully failed if it stirs you to keep on trying.[91]

Giving is the only way to see the supernatural unfold in our lives.

In the Gospel of Matthew, Jesus suggested to always believe for the impossible to take place in our lives.[92] In the realm of the supernatural one has to *"speak to the mountains"* and ask nature to move. One has to take on the impossibility.

Released By Our Giving

When did the supernatural flow in the story? Whose oil and flour was it to begin with? The widow needed to first empty her resources before her miracle happened. The only way for the widow to see the supernatural is to release the oil and flour causing it to flow unceasingly.

104

We must similarly learn to empty our "oil" and "flour" first. Our contemporary world teaches us to take, and take a lot more. The more we have, we more we will have. God's system is the exact opposite. He says to give and then it will be given back to you.[93] Giving is the only way to see the supernatural unfold in our lives.

It is about a having a generous spirit. It is about a generous attitude and disposition in life creating a conducive environment where God can trigger a release of the miraculous.

So today, do not stop giving because others within your life or circle of influence fail to give to you. Do not stop loving because others within your relationships and circle of friendship fail to love you. Let your generous spirit abound. Let it spread far and wide. Let it be the foundation upon which God brings the supernatural alongside your existence. You will begin to experience the invisible intervening hand of God in your own life.

Back To The Widow

The widow released the unexpected in her life by giving. She sacrificed her last paltry meal creating an environment for God to intervene and release his blessing. There was no immature demand for comparison or fairness. There was no demand for understanding or prior knowledge of what God was doing. She was not offended because the prophet asked unreasonably for her to feed him ahead of her son. She was truly outside the box.

In seeing the supernatural, we must avoid being boxed in. We must look beyond the natural and allow God to own and work the process without maintaining an "imposition" and expecting God's processes to be tailored to our convenience or suited to our whim and fancy. In releasing all, we will receive the best in store for us – a touch of the supernatural.

"Surprisingly, the Christian faith today is perceived as disconnected from the supernatural world – a dimension that the vast majority of outsiders believe can be accessed and influenced."

David Kinnaman, *Unchristian: What a New Generation Really Thinks about Christianity...and Why It Matters*

Chapter 14

Experiencing God

In our modern world, many people feel disconnected with God. God seems far away. Sometimes when we most needed him, he seems absent. We hear of people telling us how close God is to them or what wonderful miracles are abounding and we wonder, "How did they do it? How did they trigger it?" I mean some of our experiences are just the opposite. There are times when we felt that our desperate prayers were bouncing off the ceiling, let alone see the invisible happens.

Is an encounter or an experience with God something strange, isolated and not always attainable?

Do you wonder if it is possible for a person to have an intimate relationship with God? Can an individual experience God similar to what the great Saints did in the past? Can a person not just know the deeds of God but also his ways?[94] Is an encounter or an experience with God something strange, isolated and not always attainable? Or is it something within our grasp, totally attainable for everyone if we understand the basis for such a relationship or for his manifest presence to be found in our midst?

Moses, the Old Testament character, shows the best biblical example of God's experiences. They Bible says, *"The Lord would speak to Moses face to face, as a man speaks with his friend."*[95] But Moses was human like us. Moses had all the shortcomings of any individual person. King David is another example. He was said to be *"a man after God's own heart."*[96] David too was straddled with failures, had plenty of personal weaknesses and lived what we would call a very tumultuous life.

These men were human in more ways than one. They were as earth bound as we are today. Yet they both experienced an intimacy with God and encountered the supernatural on numerous occasions. What are their secrets?

The Apostle James suggests that we should *"come near to God and he will draw near to you."*[97] This "drawing near" is crucial to an intimate relationship and personal experiences with God. Moses and David knew how to "draw near" to God. Both men understood the basis for relationship with God. They both knew how to experience God, no matter the circumstances of the twists and turns of their life's journey. Theirs were a journey of knowing and experiencing God. In contrast, in our modern Christianity we know more about God than we know God.

They both knew how to experience God, no matter the circumstances or the twists and turns of their life's journey.

I call this a gap between knowledge and experience. This gap must be bridged if we are to naturally experience God. I also see the requirement of four basic human behaviours from one who is seeking a touch of the supernatural to bridge this gap.

Adoration

This is more than purely worship or reverence. It is an emotional response to God. We cannot have intimacy with God without having feelings about the relationship. The love and the manifest presence of God is not merely an intellectual or knowledge process, it is to be felt and reciprocated. God gives us feelings so that we could adore him. This sense of adoration is similar to my adoring something or someone I love. Hence I find my two grandchildren wholly adorable! What this means is that I am completely taken up in my emotions for them. I feel good about them. I feel love and tenderness with and for them.

Our emotional response to God often involves a deep sense of trust. This capacity to adore allows us to feel fine even when things are not exactly going our way. Because we are so in love with the Creator we quickly discover that we do not need everything in our life to be right and perfect. We can accept the difficult passages of our life knowing and feeling that God is honorable and trustworthy. I am not suggesting that we ignore our pain or problem in our emotions with God. Quite the opposite actually. In the closeness of that adoration, we bring our sorrows to him. God then inevitably walks us through the pain and the issue and out of that birth an intervening hand of the invisible God.

Adoration, with its capacity for trust tolerates apparent contradiction and discomfort in life. It brings a sense of wellness, joy, peace and laughter even if circumstances do not because we know that God has our best interests at heart. It is intentional behaviour. It is an emotional response to God's love, tender-heartedness and nearness. This is worship from the heart. Yet this worship goes beyond mere emotion, it involves discipline and a determination within our feelings to stay committed to him. If you learn to adore God, you will find him everywhere, in good and bad times, in strength and weakness.

We cannot have intimacy with God without having feelings about the relationship.

Most people want to hear from God and in my ministry I have been asked this so often, "How do you hear from God?" or "Do you hear from God?" Truth is, we hear much less but we experience God much more. Our ability to adore him produces a conducive environment where God appears more often than we realise and the result is the unavoidable happenings of spiritual phenomena in our life.

Affection

Affection is more than just emotion. It involves the mind.

This second behavioural requirement involves loving God with our mind. Affection is more than just emotion. It involves the mind. When you are affectionate to an individual, you cannot stop thinking about that person. He or she occupies your mind all the time. You are mentally engaged all the time, even if the person is not physically near you.

Our love for God must be more than just emotion. We need to love the Lord with our minds, which means we need to let him occupy and form our thoughts. It is to mentally engage, thinking, reflecting and forming thoughts that cause us to be affectionate toward the Lord God. Hence Jesus said we are to "*love the Lord your God with all your heart and with all your soul and with all your mind*".[98] The Apostle Paul counseled us to "*demolish arguments and every pretension that sets itself up against the knowledge of God, and we take captive every thought to make it obedient to Christ*".[99] We capture our thoughts through affection.

A central way to show affection is to meditate on the goodness of God's nature and the direction he takes in our life. Meditation is not scary as it sounds. It is merely thinking deeply about something. One takes time to meditate to reflect and ruminate about who God is and what he means to you.

Meditation is really "quality thinking time". It is a time where we invite the Holy Spirit to bring revelation, wisdom and clarity to our thought processes. It is thinking deeply about where God is taking you, what his plans are, what ideas are being introduced into your thought life and where God is taking you into the future. Meditation is vital to intimacy, connectivity and experiences with God. By engaging a loving God with our mind, we develop an affectionate confidence about Him. We create an unbroken fellowship by being God-conscious in our mind. And this in turn permits the introduction of spiritual phenomena into our existence.

Appreciation

Connecting with God also involves deep appreciation. In all things, we must give thanks. It is part of our human DNA that we can be naturally grateful. For example, if you eat a great meal in a restaurant, you would voice your compliments. It's just natural! If someone gives you a beautiful sweater for Christmas, you would say thanks for the gift. If someone scores a touchdown for our team, what are we really doing when we stand up, pump the air and scream our voices coarse? We are showing our deep appreciation. If pastor preaches a great sermon, we would say so! If someone wins a gold medal, or overcomes a daunting deficit to win, we jump in celebration and gratefulness. We are thankful to be a part of their historic moment.

Thanksgiving is not just for the occasion, an event or the spectacular, it should be an everyday occurrence.

So when was the last time, you jump up and down and scream your voice grainy

111

because you experience God in the ordinary? Many of our miraculous are found in the mundane, precisely because we know how to appreciate. *"In everything give thanks; for this is God's will for you in Christ Jesus."*[100]

Our experiences with God carry a voice. Christians should be vocal about the things of God particularly in our praise and gratitude. Thanksgiving is not just for the occasion, an event or the spectacular, it should be an everyday occurrence. It is character. Real experience with intimacy and the resulting spiritual phenomenal cannot be hidden. It transforms us from the inside out. To get there, however, we have to live with a mind captivated by God.

This behaviour is powerfully enabling. Gratitude improves our health and personality. Our ability to appreciate God and indeed to appreciate other facets of our lives makes us an optimistic person.[101] Appreciation is indeed a channel God uses to draw individuals closer to him. Thus the Psalmist King was able to testify that God *"inhabits in the praises of his people"*.[102]

Abiding

Abiding then is the capacity to sit still and trust God for our miracle.

Finally, experiencing God involves an ability to abide or to be steadfast in the relationship. Abiding means we value and honor our relationship with God above all others. So we stay resolute and committed to it.

Hence, spousal relationships are frequently kept unassumingly by the capacity of the parties to abide in each other. In other words the tenacity to work and build each other without much fanfare. It is a commitment to stay faithful no matter

112

what, leading to a stable relationship and the couple to enjoy the fruits of a strong marriage.

Abiding then is the capacity to sit still and trust God for our miracle. It is also the ability to accept the routine and the mundane. It is part of the process of being faithful trusting God to reach down and turn the mundane into divine, the routine into the miraculous and the ordinary into the extraordinary.[103] It is an ability not to run ahead of God. Abiding allows time, space and grace to work its ways through the issues and challenges of our life. It allows a power to stay and wait for God to bring forth a resolution to our problem. Do you know why many Christians do not experience God or worse fall away from God? This is because they did not know how to abide. We are conditioned to be too impatient, too demanding, too aggravated and too quick on the move even if speed is not always the best option.

Scripture is clear about the power of abiding. Stay and wait long enough and you will begin to experience the invisible hand of God. Jesus said, "*Abide in me, and I in you, as the branch cannot bear fruit of itself unless it abides in the vine, so neither can you unless you abide in me.*"[104] When we stay steadfast and keep our consciousness focused on God, our faith increases exponentially inviting the supernatural to abound.

More Than Knowledge

Getting connected to God and experiencing the supernatural is not just an intellectual exercise. It is not mere knowledge or a sound theological concept. Experiencing God involves the heart which is the seat of all human activity. It involves an emotional response to God. This affection of the heart and mind is not about emotionalism but you cannot adore God or for that matter anyone or anything without engaging the emotion. It is perfectly normal to be emotive about the divine. This is called being passionate and passion brings out the extraordinary.

"I am realistic – I expect miracles."

Wayne W. Dyer

Chapter 15

Is Perception Reality?

One of the great acts of the Prophet Elijah took place at Mt. Carmel where he called down fire upon the altar of Baal and then proceeded to slaughter 400 prophets of Baal.

I have been to Mt. Carmel in Israel and stood on top of this mountain at the likely spot where the event was to have taken place thousand of years ago. The mountain is very strategic in that you actually see all sides of the nation; from the Mediterranean Sea on the coast to Mt. Hermon, Israel's highest snow capped mountain on the Golan Heights, to the Samarian desert and the Judean desert stretching south towards the City of Jerusalem. From the top, you have a clear view of the entire Yizrael Valley or better known as the Armageddon.

At the top of that ancient mountain, God was demonstrating his dominion. He seemed to be showing the old prophet his authority over the land! But after the miracle took place, scriptures tell us that Elijah was fleeing for his life because the King's wife, Jezebel swore to kill him for what he did on that mountain. He fled to the desert, in hiding and asking God to let him die. Elijah was in depression. He was so discouraged because he thought he was the only godly prophet or godly man around in the whole nation.

However Elijah's perception was not reality. He thought he was the last prophet. He thought he was alone, holding the fort. He could not see what God was doing. God told him that there were actually 7,000 others in the land who had not bowed down to Baal nor kissed his image.[105] What a discrepancy in perception and reality.

This is often the case for mortals. We look at our situations and based on the obvious circumstances quickly conclude that reality must be of a certain predictable result. The problem seems insurmountable. It looks impossible. The outcome is likely to be detrimental and so on. But God says, "No, you do not see what I see or what I know or what I am doing. The situation is very different to what you are perceiving."

In other words, God may have a different reality to our perception. Our views may be flawed as we may have compromised the situation with our fears and unbelief. We see the event developing and we conclude that all is lost because it is simply impossible. The truth is that what is impossible with man is very possible with God.

The truth is that what is impossible with men is very possible with God.

Our contemporary world is full of distraction and confusion. Our culture, society's expectation and norm may dislodge and distract our attention from what God is trying to do. We can be so easily dissuaded that we too, like Elijah, may be fleeing for our lives for the wrong reasons.

This begs the question: how do I align my perception with God's reality? Three underlying principles are needed if we are to see differently and filter accurately our perception with God's reality.

Understanding What God Has Given You

This is called the mandate. John the Baptist, in the Gospel of John, understood this principle powerfully. When asked if he was the Messiah, he replied, *"A man can receive only what is given him from heaven."*[106] John understood his role in life and in the kingdom of God. He understood his mandate. He came to pave the way for the Messiah; he was not the Messiah. His ministry on earth was very brief (lost his life for speaking the truth) yet Jesus described his life as *"Among those born of women there has not risen anyone greater than John the Baptist."*[107]

Once we understand what God has given us, we can walk free in our calling. We have the mandate and with that comes the authority and the anointing. It is in this generic atmosphere that we are likely to see and experience the miraculous. Also we will have no hang-ups. We do not take offence easily. What others say or do or should do or should not do would not entangle us. We are secure in ourselves.

We have the mandate and with that comes the authority and the anointing.

Hence, if we are called to greatness, we will thrive in greatness. If we are given much, we will thrive with much. If we are called to lead, we will thrive in leadership. Whatever the mandate is, no matter how difficult the journey or the sacrifices needed; the process would be a joyous, fulfilling, enriching and a successful one.

But if we strive to walk in a role that God never gave us, it will result in frustration, hurts, disappointments, offences and failures. Having finished Law School, I can assuredly tell you that if you are not called to do such schooling mid-career, do not attempt it, as the load is incredibly huge. The schooling, the work, the stress, the journey will strain you or at the very least may be detrimental to your health and life.

This principle requires one to have a willingness to submit, adjust and to accept a lessor role as long as it is in fit with the mandate. What God has in store for us may be quite different to what we have in mind. We may be less successful than our friends. We may have to give more. We may have to settle for less.

This run counter culture to our society because we live in a world where everyone wants to be on top. Few people want to play second fiddle. Everyone seemly is entitled to a right or to be served. Everyone wants to be the winner and everyone wants to lead.

Did you realise that Jesus never had an issue with his mandate? He knew who he was. For example, when his integrity was questioned on numerous occasions, he did not set out to prove his honesty. He knew that character is not something you need to prove. It is one that is embedded in his mandate. Instead his integrity is something to be discerned. He knew the truth would eventually be found. He was not defensive about himself and the work he was doing.

Did you realise that Jesus never had an issue with his mandate? Adjustments to our understanding of what has been given to us is required if our perception and reality are seriously entangled and distorted. And unless we willingly submit and obey what God has positioned us for life, we will be missing some very important ingredients in life. God may be the missing piece in our lives even though he seemingly is with us; after all as Christians we do believe in Jesus, we go to church and we give and serve the Lord.

We must align our life with the mandate if we are to bridge the gap between our perception and God's reality; if we are to experience spiritual phenomenal.

Discovering your Gift

But unless you come to grip with your dominant gift and build your life around it, you will always miss the "fit".

It is not what others believe about you that matters because opinions can changed. It is what you believe about yourself that really counts. What and where are you primarily gifted? That gifting is your strength and the wherewithal to draw the right conclusions in life. Your primary belief about yourself and your gifting is the key to aligning your perception and God's reality for you.

All of us are built with a capacity for more, matter of fact much more than we realise. Whatever we are currently doing, we all have the capacity to improve, to do better, to discover and thrive in our gifting. The wisest man once asked, "*Do you see a man skilled in his work? He will serve before kings; he will not serve before obscure man.*"[108] Discover your gift and the skills residing in it. Use it to the max because in them you will experience the supernatural!

Gifting or talent is an interesting topic and one that is so critical in life. Gifting makes the difference between the top performers and poor performers. It can be cultivated and enhanced. But unless you come to grips with your dominant gift and build your life around it, you will always miss the "fit". Attempts in doing exploits in life would be like trying to fit square pegs into round holes.

Do not try to be somebody else. Do not emulate or be a copycat. Be an original. Stay in your strength and be celebrated. Part of the problem of our contemporary culture is the constant need to emulate someone else. Hence we have such a celebrity culture in this nation. So we blindly copy others not realising that in doing so we do not discover ourselves and we exist outside the "fit". And we wonder why God does not turn up in our life!

I have met people who are wonderfully gifted, done great exploits, been through a great inspiring career, yet looked at themselves as if they accomplished nothing in life. In their time of crisis, they fret incessantly, no wherewithal whatsoever to bring their skills and gifts to bear on their situation. They got discouraged, began to listen to negative voices and basically threw their hands up in surrender. They literally despaired for life. Be inspired by others by all means, but discover and know your gift because in them you will see the miraculous.

Relax And Trust God

How do you align perception and reality when the gap is often humongous? When everything else points south and you desire and believes for north, how do you bridge this gap?

The gap between perception and reality is bridged by faith. The gap between the impossible and all the possibilities of the future is bridged by our capacity to relax and trust God for his timely intervention. To the ancient nation of Israel, God asked them to sit back, relax and see the glory of God as he took them out of Egypt, across the desert wilderness of the Sinai, crossed the Red Sea into southwestern Saudi Arabia, up north into the mountains of Moab

The gap between the impossible and all the possibilities of the future is bridged by our capacity to relax and trust God for his timely intervention.

and Edom (now north western Jordan) – protected them, fought for them, fed them, watered them and saved them, and they are still a great nation today.

Trust God for the divine. This is almost stating the obvious and I hope you are not offended that I would provide such a silly obvious exhortation. This is perhaps the most powerful principle for life – being able to have the peace of God within our hearts and to trust God for all situations.

In life we unavoidably encounter fear, natural rational fear but also many times irrational fear and unnecessary suspicions. Scriptures actually call these fears "imaginations" and the modern man has plenty of that. The Apostle Paul has a simple approach to manage this tension in our modern life. He advocates casting these imaginations down.[109]

What if you just relax and let God be God.

I wrote in earlier chapter that as a generation we are too clever for our own good, which also explains why our modern world is so at odds with God today. We take his silence for his death and we ignore him at every which turn. So we have in this modern world of everything that comfort and technology can give, yet there exist a highest ever depression and suicide rate, extreme wickedness, random crimes, atrocity and ever worsening dysfunction in our families! And we wonder why with all our modern laws, humanistic beliefs and astonishing technology, we are going backwards not forward.

Trust God for divine intervention. What if you just relax and let God be God. Let him show you his glory. Do all you can, then relax and trust him for the miraculous. You will be surprised when you are relaxed and at peace within yourself how fast the perception and reality starts to marry in your life.

Drawing Conclusions

Be careful not to draw conclusions about your life or your situation that may not be based on fact or truth or what the Word of God promises. God always has a plan for his people that we do not know about. Ask God to give you a glimpse of his reality in place of yours.

The gap between perception and reality, the impossible and feasible is bridged by faith. Put it this way, you could carry the burden of struggling through life or permit God to carry it. The choice is yours. Whatever the difficulties, it is good to trust in faith because God is the ultimate! He rules in the affairs of man.[110]

As mentioned before, if you are one of the many people agonising over persistent issues and challenges that require a miracle to happen, keep in mind that God owns the process of the miraculous. His reality is the only reality. It is not over till he says it is over. We may not be sure how God will do it as there are thousands of ways in which he leads his people – through delays, detours, unexpected opportunities, miracles, unanswered and answered prayers, sudden opening and closing of doors, inner impressions and a still small voice.[111] Therefore do not give up hope because God has proven to be far beyond anything anyone could imagine.

The way you see Jesus affects your faith and expectation, so ensure that you sow the seed for the miraculous by trusting God's reality and not your own perception of the situation.

"In the world of miracles, you ask the impossible."

Gavriil Stiharul

Acknowledgment

I am grateful for each and every person whose miracle I am telling. They are awesome stories of inspiration, purpose and destiny. They have been generous in allowing others to catch a glimpse of what God has done in their lives. They are, anonymously or otherwise, eager to give God all the glory for the great things He has done!

My editors worked very diligently. They have gone the second mile in promoting my efforts to bring this book to print so that there is a lasting inspiration for my reading community. So to Jasphia Tan thank you for editing, reviewing and reading the script in spite of your busy lives and myriad of commitments.

To my wife, Dorothy Teo who has stood by me through 38 years of marriage and over the last eleven years of ministry, three years of Law School, the constant ministry travels and many more other commitments, I am thankful.

To the Lord God we give you all the glory!

About The Author

Steven Teo was born of Chinese parents in Singapore in 1952. He is an accountant by training. In 1991 Steven completed his MBA at Monash University, Australia. Subsequently, he graduated from the International Management Development Institute (IMD), Switzerland in Executive Education.

Seeking to add a new dimension to his work and ministry, he recently completed Law School and commenced his legal practical training and internship with an established Law firm. He is now an accredited mediator with the Australian Mediation Association.

Steven had been in the corporate world for many years. He was the Chief Executive Officer (CEO) of the Singapore Office of an international insurance Group for seven years. He later assumed additional responsibility as CEO of their Malaysian operation as well. Concurrently he was the Chairman of a Practice Board for the Asia Pacific Region and represented that region at the Global commercial Board in Switzerland.

Before starting his itinerary ministry, Steven completed his theological training at a Bible College in Australia. He is now an ordained minister with the Full Gospel Churches of Australia and is the Founding Director of *Dream4enations Ministries Incorporated*, a tax-exempt Christian ministry based in Melbourne.

Parallel to his strategic work with corporation and ministry to churches, Steven has an on-going mentoring program for pastors, business and professional individuals. The *"InSight"* program as it has come to be known is a subscription-based ministry that aims to bring clarity of thought and focus to those who are subscribers. He believes that God intentionally entrusted him with a set of skills, resources and practical experiences to provide clarity of thought leadership ministry.

Steven and his wife, Dorothy live in Melbourne, Australia, together with his son Joses and wife Nadia who have given them a pair of adorable grandchildren.

No Pain No Gain

We are often inspired by stories of how people prospered despite their very difficult circumstances. They battled against great odds to become a success story.

Across the globe, in every direction, in every nation whether rich or poor, there exist stories of unlikely individuals who made it good. They are people who should not be victorious and should not have accomplished given their situations but they did.

On first look, these are people born into the wrong place, the wrong time and perhaps even the wrong color. They have nothing going for them. Everything appears to be against them. Life gives every reason to succumb to their situation, to call it quits and accept their status quo. They have all the grounds to be angry and to put blame on their parents, loved ones, friends, society, politics, government, schools and perhaps even the church. But they did not. They were casted for failures yet they triumphed.

Who are these people? Why are they able to swim against the tide? What make them so different? Are they the exceptions or are they the norm? What are the critical factors that help them turn things around? Read about them in this book. All of these are real life stories of people who stood against the odds. And won.

Paperback 9 780977518098

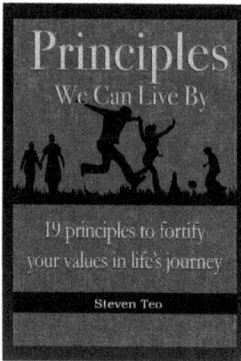

*Other Resources by
Pastor Steven Teo*

Principles We Can Live By

For many years, I have had the privilege of working with and guiding incredible leaders across nations. The process had allowed me opportunity to articulate values that are core to my personal belief system and my endeavors for the kingdom of God. As these values, which were premised on principles had benefitted many. I was encouraged to put them to print by crafting this book for the benefit of many more.

Assembled within these pages are nineteen value-driven principles. Whilst they written in alphabetical order and may be best to read in the order – each value-driven principle can be appreciated and appropriated on its own, and applied to life.

I am trusting that these principles will help you fortify your own values in life's journey.

ISBN 978 0 9803778 1 1

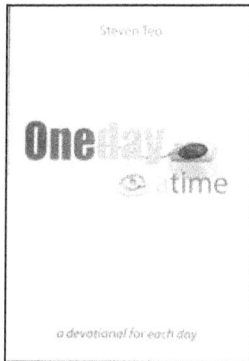

One Day @ A Time

"Success consists of a series of little daily victories."

- Laddie F. Hutar

In this book, Pastor Steven reminds us of the importance of spending time every day with God; connecting and interacting with the presence of the Holy Spirit.

This daily time even if it is a few minutes is a great way to begin the day. It will set the pace for the day, allow your mind to establish a pre-requisite link with God before you do anything else. This is a fruitful time to set a more positive tone to the inevitable challenges of daily living thereby ensuring the probability of little victories.

This devotion draws from Pastor Steven's sermons preached over the last five years of global ministries, camps, workshops and seminars to provide a fresh and renewing word from each day.

Paperback 9 7809803778 0 4

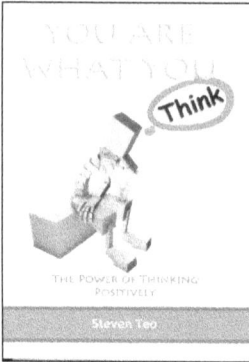

You Are What You Think

The Power of Thinking Positively

Foreword by Rev. Richard F. Warner

This book is not another "hypey" attempt to jump on the positive thinking bandwagon, but rather it is a practical and genuine goldmine of ideas that Steven has proven with his own life and now shares freely from his experience. Together with some gem quotes, appropriate biblical examples, tinged with a dash of humor, this book is a must read for all who yearn to make their life count and finish well.

Rev. Richard F. Warner
President
Lighthouse Christian Centre and College
Melbourne, Australia

Paperback 9 7809775180 7 4

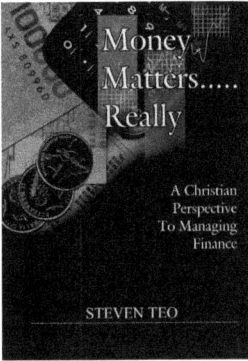

Other Resources by
Pastor Steven Teo

Money Matters....Really

A Christian perspective to managing finance

Foreword by Kenny Koay

This book has the power to change not only your financial life but also your whole life. It will bring fullness of life as you read and put into practice the principles that are taught here. You will find freedom and blessings not only for yourself and your family but also for your community and your church.

You will also find that this book is extremely practical and backed by sound understanding of the Bible. Pastor Steven used his gift of clarity to unpack timeless biblical financial wisdom, bringing relevance and practicality for the twenty-first century generation.

Kenny Koay
Business Executive
Melbourne, Australia

Paperback 0-9775180 4 3

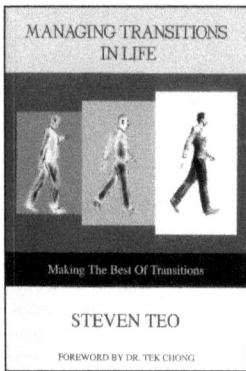

Managing Transitions In Life

Making The Best of Transitions

A book to help you succeed in managing life's transitions.

Foreword by Dr. Tek Chong

In this book, Steven shares his accumulated insight from his personal journey of change. He records his transition from the business world into the church and then out again into the marketplace. His writing is clear-cut and well supported by sound research. I enjoyed his many interesting anecdotes.

I wish there had been a similar book earlier. It would have made my many transitions smoother and easier.

Dr. Kwong-tek Chong
A medical practitioner who transited to become Pastor of FGA Marketplace Church, Perth, WA, Australia

Paperback 0 9775180-0-0

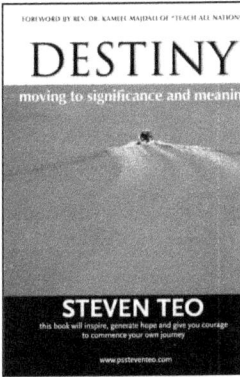

DESTINY

Moving to Significance and Meaning

This book will inspire, generate hope and give you courage to commence your own journey.

"Inspiring. Challenging. Insightful. Joyful. Triumphant. Faith-filled. Motivational.

Steven Teo is one of the most positive, encouraging and uplifting person I know. I tell him he is small on the outside, but big on the inside…generous, insightful, humble and kind. *Destiny* inspires people at any level to move from self-doubt, lack, disadvantage and challenge to abundance, generosity, influence and full potential. As you read Steven's story, you will pick up little gems along the way in his journey that will change your life and thinking. *Destiny* a must read for any person who has ever felt "God, are you sure you were right in choosing someone like me?"

Rev. Enzo Maisano
Pastor, ENJOY Church
Melbourne

Paperback 0 9775180-5-1

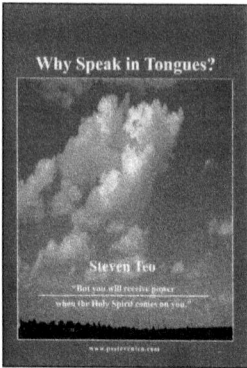

Other Resources by
Pastor Steven Teo

Why Speak in Tongues?

Is speaking in tongues important today? Is speaking in tongues a practice that is defendable?

Tongues has been debated and disputed for a long time. Some Christians believe that tongues is a contemporary gift of the Holy Spirit but do not recognize it as the initial evidence of the baptism in the Holy Spirit; neither do they believe that speaking in tongues is essential in order to be effective in spiritual gifting.

This booklet is a compilation of outlines, articles, journals, library researches and lesson notes drawn from the *"Pneumatology"* (Doctrine of the Holy Spirit) class that I attended at a Bible college in Melbourne. It deals with the issue of the importance of tongue-speaking from a biblical standpoint, how it can be used and what it does for the believer.

Pastor Steven Teo
Re-Gen Ministries Inc.
Melbourne

Paperback 0-9775180-1-9

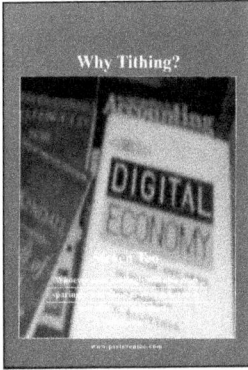

Why Tithing?

Did you know that Jesus taught more about stewardship than any other subject?

Jesus knew that for many of us, the treasure comes first! Hence, he said in Matthew 6:21, *"For where your treasure is, there your heart will be also."*

So Jesus wants our treasures to be at the right place, so that our hearts will also be there. I hope as you read this booklet, you will be encouraged by the insights to adopt a lifestyle of stewardship. It deals with the issues of tithing and the concept of lifestyle giving from a biblical standpoint, yet entirely sensitive to the difficult pastoral issue here due to the private nature of finances.

This booklet is a compilation of outlines, articles, library researches and lesson notes drawn from the *"Pastoral Ministry"* class that I attended at a Bible college in Melbourne.

Pastor Steven Teo
Re-Gen Ministries Inc
Melbourne

Paperback 0-9775180-3-5

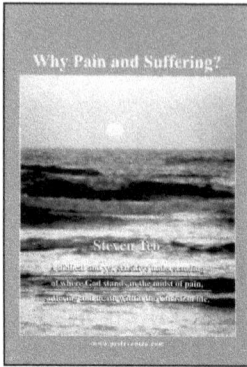

Why Pain and Suffering?

Job loves God for who God is! He said in Job 13:15, *"Though he slay me, yet will I hope in him."*

Many Christians do have a tendency to make the Christian life sound easy. We often wrongly assume or at least give the wrong impression that once we become a Christian, all our problems will be over. Where did we ever get the idea that Christians should not have problems? God is more interested in forging your character than He is in ensuring your comfort. Fact is the Christian life is never an easy one. Life constantly throws us challenges that we need to overcome.

Read this booklet and be encouraged by the insights. Make full use of the materials and utilize this resource for meeting the challenges of pain, suffering and death you may encounter, either in your own life or that of your family members, colleagues, neighbors, friends and/or acquaintances associated with you.

Pastor Steven Teo
Re-Gen Ministries Inc
Melbourne

Paperback 0-9775180-2-7

We want to hear from you. Please send your comments about this book to st@pssteventeo.com. You can also visit www.pssteventeo.com and provide feedback.
Thank you.

Notes

Chapter One
[1] 2 Timothy 3:5
[2] Psalm 84:2
[3] Roberts, Oral, *"When You See The Invisible You Can Do The Impossible"* Destiny Image, Shippensburg PA, 2002, 201
[4] Romans 4:17

Chapter Two
[5] Stanley Hauerwas – America's foremost theologian currently teaches at Duke University serving as the Gilbert T. Rowe Professor of Theological Ethics. More information is available at:
      http://divinity.duke.edu/academics/faculty/stanley-hauerwas
[6] Hebrews 11: 24-27
[7] James 4:2
[8] 1 Corinthians 2:9
[9] Jeremiah 29:11
[10] Exodus 2:11-15
[11] Exodus 3:1-2
[12] Exodus 3:12-20
[13] Hebrews 11:6
[14] 1 Samuel 17:26
[15] 1 Samuel 17:35-37
[16] Roberts, Oral, *"When You See The Invisible You Can Do The Impossible"* Destiny Image, Shippensburg PA, 2002, 6
[17] Ibid
[18] Mark 6:1-6
[19] Roberts, Oral, *"When You See The Invisible You Can Do The Impossible"* Destiny Image, Shippensburg PA, 2002, 68
[20] Hebrews 11:6

Chapter Three
[21] Luke 24:17-21
[22] Charlotte Kuchinsky, *"Miracles Are Being Witnessed Around the World"*. More information is available at:

http://voices.yahoo.com/miracles-being-witnessed-around-world-711449.html

[23] Daily Devotional - February 27, 2013 *"Blind Eyes & Burning Hearts"* More information is available at:
http://www.godtube.com/devotionals/our-daily-journey/daily-devotional-february-27-2013-blind-eyes-burning-hearts.html

[24] Eldredge, John, *"The Heart"* Thomas Nelson, Nashville, USA 2007, 246

[25] Luke 24:32

[26] Luke 24:25

[27] Luke 24:30-31

[28] Eldredge, John, *"The Heart"* Thomas Nelson, Nashville, USA 2007, 246-7

[29] Daily Devotional - February 27, 2013 *"Blind Eyes & Burning Hearts"* More information is available at:
http://www.godtube.com/devotionals/our-daily-journey/daily-devotional-february-27-2013-blind-eyes-burning-hearts.html

[30] Roberts, Oral, *"When You See The Invisible You Can Do The Impossible"* Destiny Image, Shippensburg PA, 2002, 67-8

[31] "InSight" – a mentoring and coaching ministry of Ps Steven Teo; the aim is to bring clarity and thought leadership into the lives of those who subscribe to this service thereby enabling the individuals to understand their inflection point and moving on to their next level.

[32] Daniel 4:17

[33] Hebrews 13:8

[34] Romans 4:17

[35] Romans 8:28

[36] Proverbs 4:23

Chapter Four

[37] Pastors Philip and Monica Lee are Singaporean missionaries for many years. They have been ministering the Gospel in many nations. Pastors Philip and Steven were schoolmates during their secondary school years. They grew up in the same church in Singapore.

Chapter Five

[38] This city is a UNESCO world heritage site. It has a rich trading history and multicultural heritage. It is the capital of the State of Malacca, on the west coast of Peninsular Malaysia.

[39] Pastor Albert Ong, The Awesome God Church (TAG), Klang

[40] Pastor Joanne Lee of City Community Church, Melaka

[41] Melaka is famous for its sumptuous food

[42] Teo, Steven, *"Destiny; Moving to Significance and Meaning"*, Re-Gen Ministries Inc., Melbourne, 2006, Chapter Seven

Chapter Six

[43] Pskov is the administrative center of Pskov Oblast, Russia, located about 20 kilometers east from the Estonian border, on the Velikaya River

[44] Emmanuel Faith Church

[45] 1 Corinthians 12:8

Chapter Seven

[46] Genesis 11:1-9

[47] Genesis 11:5

[48] Matthew 10:20

[49] Pseudo name to protect the identity of the individual

Chapter Eight

[50] "Underground Churches in China" estimated a conservative 155 million Christians in China. For more information is available at:
    http://www.billionbibles.org/china/how-many-christians-in-china.html

[51] Matthew 16:18

[52] James 5:13-16

[53] Kinnaman, David and Lyons, Gabe, *"Unchristian: What a New Generation Really Thinks about Christianity...and Why It Matters"* Baker Books, Grand Rapids, 2007, 121

Chapter Nine

[54] Medication for high blood lipid or high blood cholesterol

[55] Pseudo place to protect identity
[56] Pseudo place again to protect identity
[57] Adam Khoo Learning Technologies Group, Singapore
[58] The book was written by Pastor Joseph Prince of New Creation Church, Singapore
[59] Baby Goh & Jane Ng from APAC Ministries, Singapore

Chapter Ten
[60] The Full Gospel Assemblies of God Church
[61] Isaiah 53:5

Chapter Eleven
[62] Full Gospel Churches
[63] "InSight" – a mentoring and coaching ministry of Ps Steven Teo; the aim is to bring clarity and thought leadership into the lives of those who subscribe to this service thereby enabling the individuals to understand their inflection point and moving on to their next level.
[64] 1 Corinthians 11:23-26
[65] Psalm 103:5

Chapter Twelve
[66] M. Scott Peck, "*The Road Less Traveled: A New Psychology of Love, Traditional Values, and Spiritual Growth*", Touchstone Book, Simon & Schuster, 2nd Edition, 1998, 235-6
[67] Collins Gem Australian English Dictionary, Collins Sons & Co. Ltd., 1981
[68] Lionel Andrés "Leo" Messi – is an Argentine footballer who plays as a forward for FC Barcelona and the Argentina national team. He serves as the captain of his country's national football team. He is arguably one of the best players in the world, if not the best.
[69] Genesis 21:5; Hebrews 11:11-2
[70] Zacharias, Ravi, "*Recapture the Wonder*", Integrity Publishers, 2003, 25
[71] Matthew 27:39-40
[72] More information is available at:
http://www.eyewitnesstohistory.com/jewishtemple.htm
[73] More information is available at:
http://ldolphin.org/kingdom/ch9.html

[74] John 2:19-20
[75] Matthew 28:1-4
[76] Isaiah 55:8-9
[77] Mark 8:22-25
[78] The thing about common sense is that it is often not so common!
[79] Ephesians 1:17

Chapter Thirteen
[80] 1 Kings 19:9-16
[81] 1 Kings 17:12
[82] 1 Kings 17:15
[83] The Old Testament family represents a larger body that the English word suggests. The Hebrew word (*mishpachah*) was used to describe the larger patriarchal clan which included individuals related by blood, marriage, slaveship, and even animals. Occasionally even strangers or sojourners could be included in the larger household. More information is available at:
   http://www.studylight.org/dic/hbd/view.cgi?number=T2013
[84] Mark 11:24
[85] Hebrew 11:1b
[86] The Amplified Bible
[87] 1 Corinthians 2:16
[88] 1 Corinthians 2:9
[89] Victor Hugo quotes. More information is available at:
   http://www.searchquotes.com/search/Courage_Is_Not_The_Absence_Of_Fear/
[90] 2 Corinthians 1:9
[91] Gass, B., *"A Fresh Word for Today"*, Bridge-Logos Publishers, North Brunswick, 2000, 204,209
[92] Matthew 17:20
[93] Luke 6:38

Chapter Fourteen
[94] Psalm 103:7
[95] Exodus 33:11
[96] Acts 13:22
[97] James 4:8
[98] Matthew 22:37

[99] 2 Corinthians 10:5
[100] 1 Thessalonians 5:18
[101] More information is available at:
        http://happierhuman.com/benefits-of-gratitude/
[102] Psalm 22:3
[103] Minter, Kelly, *"Water into Wine, hope for the Miraculous in the Struggle of the Mundane"*, Waterbrook Press, 2004, 70
[104] John 15:4

Chapter Fifteen

[105] 1 Kings 19:18
[106] John 3:27
[107] Matthew 11:11
[108] Proverbs 22:29
[109] 2 Corinthians 10:2-5
[110] Daniel 4:17b
[111] Pritchard, Ray, *"Beyond all you could ask Or Think"*, Moody Publishers, Chicago, 2004, 120

www.ingramcontent.com/pod-product-compliance
Lightning Source LLC
Chambersburg PA
CBHW070633030426
42337CB00020B/4001